The
Toltec Path *of*
Recapitulation

The
Toltec Path *of*
Recapitulation

Healing Your Past to Free Your Soul

Victor Sanchez

Bear & Company
Rochester, Vermont

Bear & Company
One Park Street
Rochester, Vermont 05767
www.InnerTraditions.com

Library of Congress Cataloging-in-Publication Data
Sanchez, Victor.
   The Toltec path of recapitulation : healing your past to free your soul /
Victor Sanchez.
            p. cm.
   ISBN 1-879181-60-6 (pbk.)
   1. Shamanism. 2. Mental healing—Miscellanea. 3. Toltecs—Miscellanea. I. Title.
   BF1621 .S26 2001
   299 ' .792—dc21

                                                            2001003092

Printed and bound in Canada

10 9 8 7 6 5 4 3 2 1

Text design and layout by Rachel Goldenberg
This book was typeset in Deepdene with Poppl-Laudatio as the display typeface

*I dedicate this book to the memory
of that Carlos Castaneda
of the earlier years.*

Contents

Preface

It has been said that we all, at the moment of dying, have a second to see our entire life again, to relive the feelings involved in all the events we have passed through. It has been said that this final second is expanded so that we can recapitulate the meaningful events of our life.

It has been said that because of the magic of this last reliving, in that last moment we are able to put everything in balance, recapturing the beauty hidden in the simplest events: a tender flower opening its petals to the rising sun or the fresh smell of the soil after the rain. The warmth of a loved person sleeping by your side or the brilliance in the eyes of our children when they discover with amazement the extraordinary components of the world. The healing power of an embrace given in a moment of grief or the ineffable mystery of a starry night. The laughter of loved ones or the trembling feeling of a first kiss. The silent magic of the rain seen through the window or the joy of contemplating the fire in the chimney. The falling leaves of a tree, alive and dancing for a minute, enraptured by the cast of the fall wind. In other words, the extraordinary magic behind the ordinary things.

It is in that moment, at the edge of death, when we realize that we have been dead from a long time ago, and only then are we fully awake and we recover the exhilaration and overwhelming understanding of the miracle of being alive.

And then we die.

It is sad that the last recapitulation opens the eyes of our full awareness, closed until this moment. The miracle of life is revealed to us and then we fade away . . . but does it have to be like that? Is there no other way? Would it be possible, by any means, to recover such awareness of the magic and joy of being alive and to use it, not to die, but to live, *to really live?*

The answer is yes. We can perform, on purpose, the healing journey of recapitulating our lives to recover the joy and power that we had once, just by receiving the miracle of life.

This book is about the process of recovering passion for life. This book deals with the techniques, procedures, and results of such a process. This book is an open door into this quest. It is about you and your life, if you feel the call.

Welcome to the journey.

Victor Sanchez

Acknowledgments

M any people contributed to the existence of this book. I want to express my gratitude to all of them.

Thanks to all the people—instructors and participants—in our workshops on recapitulation from 1984 to the present.

Thanks to Manolo Cetina, for his companionship and the value of his vision and work, which contributed so much to making this work possible.

Thanks to Armando Cruz and the rest of the AVP staff members, in Mexico and abroad, for their support, creativity, and courage to keep fighting in the spirit of the new Toltec warriors.

I want to express my gratitude to Elaine Sanborn for her meticulosity and care in the editing and work of this book; and to all the good people of Inner Traditions • Bear & Company, from Ehud Sperling, the visionary entrepreneur, to those who work to produce the books. They are all committed to making this world a better place in which to live.

Special thanks from my heart to Jody Spehar for her support in proofing, criticizing, and commenting on this work. But thanks to her mainly for the warmth of her love and friendship that accompanied me during the not-so-easy days of writing these pages.

Thanks to all those humans, animals, trees, planets, and stars that constitute my family, for giving me the chance to learn that the warrior's path is nonsense and goes nowhere if not nurtured by the unfathomable force of love.

Introduction

This work is part of my report from twenty years of research in the field of indigenous knowledge and shamanism. Recapitulation is a powerful technique, developed in the field of what I call shamanic technology.

Since the word *shamanism* has transcended its origin among indigenous peoples from Siberia and is used so much by members of modern urban societies nowadays, it is appropriate to explain briefly how I understand that word and the way I use it.

From a superficial perspective, a shaman is that person who has the knowledge and power to deal with supernatural forces, most of the time in order to heal. Those supernatural forces could be spirits, gods, entities, energies, or God.

During the last twenty years, shamanism has changed from being an important issue for anthropologists involved in cultural research to becoming an attractive issue for nonspecialists interested in healing and spiritual growth.

Initially, our interest in shamanism had to do with the fantasy of meeting a "real shaman" to be healed or blessed by his or her supernatural powers. As the years have passed, our focus on shamanism has changed; now *we* want to be the shamans to heal others and heal the world. Books, workshops, and seminars on shamanism for that purpose are being offered extensively around the world. Many people are reading those books and attending those workshops with the fantasy of becoming a shaman, getting power, and solving the eternal need to stop being "nobody" and eventually become "somebody." This pursuit is another example of the kind of things we are willing to do because of the lack of sense in our lives.

It is interesting to notice that for the modern man the idea of shamanism is related to the idea of power: power to heal; power to change the events of life; power to bring the rain, good fortune, and so forth. My experience among indigenous peoples from Mexico, whom I call the surviving Toltecs, has shown me a very different perspective. Shamanism is related to the idea of service, rather than the idea of power.

The flesh-and-bone shamans I have known are marked by their commitment to the service of their communities as their primary feature. What's extraordinary about them is not so much how big their power is but how extreme their vocation to serve others is without asking for rewards. They don't charge for their work. Rather than having income as a result of their activities as shamans, they are the poorest among the poor ones, because besides working as hard as any other in their lives as peasants, they spend a great deal of time working hard in the service of their communities.

Because of their extreme generosity and nobility of spirit, I have always been reluctant to agree with the way the word *shamanism* is used in our modern world, where oversimplification is the rule. Nowadays, anybody who has read even a little bit about indigenous knowledge or participated in workshops on shamanism presents him- or herself as a shaman in order to sell an image that can be admired by others.

In my work giving lectures and leading seminars around the world for so long, many people (workshop organizers, media interviewers, and so forth) have tried to dress me with the title of shaman. I have never accepted that, because I know real shamans and their offering of an entire

life of service to reflect spirit, without a trace of self-importance in what
they do. Because of that, I would never dare to put myself at the same
level of those men and women of bare feet; my audiences will not be large
because I don't participate in the dance of masks, pretending to be a shaman or a *nagual*.

In my opinion, most of the time what is behind the compulsive need
to wear titles is self-importance. The need to present oneself as "I am the
one" to others has done much damage, for both the "illuminated" ones
and their followers. I know those titles are convenient for marketing and
profits, but for me freedom is a more precious value. At the end, we all die
as we have lived. Death is not impressed by our titles.

Shamans of real life are not like the perfect indigenous masters of
books. Their bodies bleed, their hearts suffer, their children get sick, their
souls cry and laugh. Indigenous shamans in the real world are facing the
violence of a time when their whole world is being devoured by the un-
bounded greed of the white man. And they are resisting. They are fighting to survive and to keep the treasure of their spiritual tradition alive—not
just for them, not even just for their children, but for the entire world,
you and me included.

What makes them so precious for humanity is that they are making
the miracle of raising themselves and their people from the existential
misery and solitude in which we live to reach and become one with the
most extraordinary force in this universe: the unspeakable, the Great
Spirit. And the most extraordinary part is that they are making this miracle
of recovering the lost unit at the same time that they are struggling with
extreme poverty. They are human beings, just like you and me, dealing
and fighting with the material world, just like you and me. But they are
able to raise themselves from the pain and confusion of the material world,
to reach the Spirit and become one with God. And the big news is that
what they do, we can do. They are showing us the way, but it is our responsibility to perform the miracle by ourselves in our own life.

My experience with shamanism has shown me that the task of the shaman has little to do with achieving individual goals. Shamans are not doing what they do as a personal issue. They are participating, together with their community, in <u>the task of remembering and keeping alive the means to return to the Spirit and live in harmony with it.</u> Those sets of procedures are called *tradition,* which is not a body of beliefs but instead <u>a body of practices.</u>

Now let's change the focus from the shaman as an individual to the shamanic experience as a possibility for everyone. While the shaman is a specific person, playing a specific role in the magical time of the rituals and ceremonies, the shamanic experience is lived and shared by all the individuals involved in the event. (In this sense the shamanic experience is both individual and collective and therefore is open to all the members of the group as long as they follow the proper procedures.)

The goal of the shamanic experience is to bring back the participants to the lost unity with the unspeakable force moving everything in the universe. The separate poles—sacred and mundane, spirit and matter, the self and "what's out there"—all <u>become one during the shamanic experience.</u> (Our two internal sides, tonal and nagual, are reintegrated and we experience <u>the unity of our double nature.</u>)

The <u>recovery of that unity is the secret promise in the Toltec symbol of the feathered serpent Quetzalcoatl.</u> The serpent represents what crawls, the tonal, the material world. The eagle represents what flies, the nagual, the Spirit. But unlike the Aztec symbol, in which the eagle is killing the serpent* the Toltec symbol of Quetzalcoatl shows how the eagle and the serpent have become one: the feathered serpent, the unity of spirit and matter, the equilibrium between tonal and nagual.

The shamanic experience is important for us, members of modern urban societies, not just because it could be exciting or fun to become a sha-

---

*The Aztec symbol may be seen in the shield of the Mexican flag: an eagle devouring a serpent over a red fruit cactus. The height of the Aztec civilization represented just two hundred years of history in Mexico, from 1325, when the Aztecs founded their capital, Tenochtitlán (now Mexico City), to 1521, when the Spanish began the destruction of their world.

man. The shamanic experience is deadly important because our lack of appropriate means to reconnect ourselves with the Spirit is causing a continual process of self-destruction, for us as individuals and as a species.

Because of this, my work for all these years has been to try to create a bridge between our modern societies and the shamanic experiences kept alive among indigenous peoples. I am convinced that the major disease of our time is the lack of experiences in which we may remember and live again our hidden awareness (the other self) and the sacred connection we have with everything surrounding us.

We need shamanic practices that are appropriate for our time and our society. It would not be enough just to try to imitate the rituals and procedures of indigenous peoples. Shamanism and tradition are a series of practices and techniques to manipulate and heighten awareness. But the specific expression of these technologies is and should always be in accordance with the specific features of the people who are going to use them in a specific time and place. This means that while the shamanic practices of indigenous peoples should be related to the features of their way of life as peasants who live in close contact with nature, our practices should be related to the kind of world and life we have in modern cities.

Our effort in AVP, the New Toltequity,* has been to develop methods and procedures for the people of the modern world, so they can complete by themselves the shamanic jump to the other side of themselves and to the other side of reality. The reason for this journey through the shamanic experience is that there is no health without completion. Only by recovering and integrating the experiences corresponding to our double nature can we reach what constitutes our natural rights: power, health, and freedom.

What I call shamanic technology introduces the results of our experience researching and developing the modern expressions of the shamanic

---

*Find a short explanation of the AVP organization in chapter 1, page 17. For a more thorough explanation of the workshops, see appendix B.

experience. *The Toltec Path of Recapitulation* introduces the practice of recapitulation, which I consider to be one of the first and main steps for a serious process of healing and self-liberation.

The Use of the Word *Toltec* and the Indigenous Roots of Recapitulation

The word *Toltec* has been abused in so many ways that a clarifying comment is needed here.

As a Mexican person and member of a tradition whose roots come from the ancient Toltec (a historical ethnic group from Mexico), I have been sensitive to the strange use of this name, such as applying it to people who have come from other planets, from Atlantis, or from other dimensions. Such theories are a misrepresentation of the historical existence of the ancient Toltecs and the current existence of indigenous peoples who keep alive the ancient traditions of the Toltecs.

I understand the positive intention that many people may have in using the word *Toltec* to refer to a person of knowledge, but at the same time I think it is very important to have a special respect for the historical Toltecs and the surviving Toltecs by not creating confusion around the identity of this group. Respect for a culture that has served humanity by preserving and sharing its sacred technology for heightened awareness is also demonstrated by consciously not misrepresenting those of this culture. This misrepresentation often occurs in spiritual books in which Toltecs are characterized by the imaginations and expectations of non-indigenous spiritual seekers.

Of course, the intentions of the writers of these books are positive—by writing books related to those indigenous people who are connected to the Toltec tradition, they are, on the one hand, calling attention to and promoting respect and appreciation of these people. On the other hand, however, these books may be contributing to misunderstanding these people by substituting their voice, knowledge, and world vision with one that is not their own.

Because of this, it is important for me to make clear that the recapitulation techniques presented in this book are *inspired by* ancient Toltec practices, including some that are still followed by indigenous peoples of Mexico such as the Wirrarika. As far as I know, however, these techniques were not performed in this way by the ancient Toltecs, nor are they performed today by the surviving Toltec.

There are roots of the practice of recapitulation to be found among the Toltecs of the past as well as other ancient indigenous groups. *Tlacentlalia* is a word in Nahuatl (the language of the Toltec, Aztec, and many other indigenous groups in Mexico) that was translated by Alonso de Molina,* a sixteenth-century Catholic friar, as "gathering together the sins, bringing them to memory." It is obvious that the energetic healing process of recapitulation was unknown to him; he relates the same process to the concept of sin. The resulting practice was *teochihua,* which de Molina translates as "releasing the sins," and which we understand today as a healing catharsis.

This kind of practice can be found among the Wirrarika people of the present who have in their ritual the practice of telling the history of their lives, as well as whatever may be considered a sin or emotional pain, to Grandfather Fire. This practice implies an energetic exchange that takes place beyond verbal communication and is followed during their sacred pilgrimages; during moments of intimacy with the fire in the *kalihuey,* or ceremonial center in their communities; or anywhere else where a ritual fire is ignited.

These kinds of indigenous practices of the past and present are the roots of the techniques developed by me and my team in nearly twenty years of research.† Our techniques are a modern expression of

---

*Fray Alonso de Molina, *Vocabulario en lengua Castellana y Mexicana,* edición facsimilar (Madrid: 1944).

†The influence of part of the ideas of Carlos Castaneda requires a separate comment, which you can find at the end of this work, in About the Sources of This Book.

these ancient self-healing practices. In other words, they should be understood as modern or new Toltec techniques.

To make this completely clear, we can establish a simple distinction between all three kinds of Toltecs:

- The *ancient Toltecs* were a specific indigenous group from central Mexico, existing sometime between the seventh and twelfth centuries, whose spiritual influence on many other indigenous peoples of the past was the greatest in the Mexican pre-Hispanic indigenous world. Despite the dark, bloody tales that the European conquerors created around the Toltecs, this group represented the height of spiritual, cultural, and technological development in ancient Mexico. The current presence in the Mexican territory of indigenous peoples who are their spiritual heirs can be proved without doubt.
- The *surviving Toltecs* refers to those indigenous peoples who have kept alive the tradition of the ancient Toltecs and whom I have been involved with, as I have described in *Toltecs of the New Millennium.*
- The *new Toltecs* are both indigenous and nonindigenous peoples who are working to keep the Toltec tradition alive, not only in the indigenous world, but in the nonindigenous world as well. The new Toltecs are committed to following the path of the ancient and surviving Toltecs by creating specific and appropriate procedures to fit the needs of our modern, urban societies. It could be said that we are opening new paths, following the footprints of the ancient Toltecs.

About the Structure
of This Book

This is a book oriented to practice. It presents the results of long research into a process of self-healing of the energetic body that effects major changes and benefits in the practitioner's life.

I have organized this book into two parts: Part 1, devoted to theory, and Part 2, devoted to practice, the latter being the larger section of the work. Since I am a man basically oriented more to action than to thoughts or words (I can understand clearly those readers who want to go directly to the exercises (skipping the theoretical part), especially those who are familiar in one way or another with the theme of recapitulation.)

On the one hand, I understand that kind of haste to enter into the practice. On the other hand, I cannot make here the same suggestion that I did in my book *The Teachings of Don Carlos,* where I told my readers that it was okay to skip chapters and go directly to the reading and practice of those techniques that were more attractive to them. On the contrary, in this book I highly recommend not skipping chapters but reading them all in the order they are presented, because each step will be really understood only in the light of the following ones.

The reason is that this book deals basically with a single area of work and all its component techniques. Part 1 deals with two main goals:

1. To explain what recapitulation is, why it is such a valuable practice, and what we can get from its practice
2. To provide the general sense of understanding and commitment that should accompany the process of practicing recapitulation

Even if you are already willing to do recapitulation, you are going to need the information provided in the first part of this book. Additionally, in this part you will hear about the evidences, testimonies, and results of many of those who have practiced recapitulation throughout the years of our research.

And at the end of this part I have included a comment of prevention about the exceptional cases when recapitulation is not recommended.

Part 2 is devoted basically to the presentation and instructions for practicing recapitulation and all its sub-techniques. The AVP Ten-Steps Technique for Recapitulation is presented here and is the main content of this book.

At the end of this part you will find a complementary chapter that deals with the following:

- Special techniques to recapitulate single events without using the recapitulation box, instead of recapitulating series of events about our entire life as we do with the main technique.
- The whole set of special breathing techniques used during recapitulation exercises.
- Additional practices to balance your life, after the introduction of the changes achieved through recapitulation. Here we will deal with field exercises in nature, saving energy, cultivating well-being, and so forth.
- Information about the activities and workshops that AVP groups organize around the world.

Now you have an idea about the itinerary. Enjoy the trip!

PART 1

The What, Why, and How of Recapitulation

1

Preliminaries and First Approach to Recapitulation

The Outline

In simple words recapitulation is a procedure of self-healing that is done by reliving the events of our past in such a way that we are able to restore our own being from the damage that many of those events left in us.

This damage is usually expressed as repetitive emotional conflicts. The persistence of the routines of our personality that drain our vital energy comes from this energetic damage as well. Recapitulation is the medicine for that disease. In terms of energy it could be said that recapitulation is the series of energetic procedures that restore our field of energy from the damage received in the past.

The consequence of recapitulation is recovery of the state of completeness that we had at the moment of our birth. In practical terms it implies recovering the freedom of choosing how to be and how to live, instead of endlessly repeating the exhausting internal routines established in our past.

I have written about recapitulation and described the basic technique in my book *The Teachings of Don Carlos.** Nevertheless, ten years have

*Victor Sanchez, *The Teachings of Don Carlos* (Santa Fe, N. Mex.: Bear & Company, 1995).

passed from the time when the first draft of the book was written. During those ten years a great deal has happened regarding our research in recapitulation. From the first design of the technique described in my first book to the current techniques, much has changed, and the procedure now has a much more refined design. The experience of those ten years—working with recapitulation, meeting with successes, and sometimes making mistakes to learn from them—has taken us to the moment of presenting to the world what we call New Discoveries in Recapitulation and The AVP Ten-Steps Technique for Recapitulation.

All this experience, these changes, the amazing positive results we have found through working with recapitulation, and the perception that recapitulation is one of the most efficient and transformational processes a human being can undertake have been my motivation to write this book.

The Roots of Recapitulation

The roots of recapitulation are lost in time. Legends and living practices among indigenous peoples, descendants of the ancient Toltecs, speak about the enormity of the knowledge developed by the ancient habitants of Tula and other Toltec populations. Different recapitulation-like experiences are still practiced among their descendants.

The indigenous practice of telling one's life story to Grandfather Fire is a simple but deep way of recapitulation. It is also an example of how the awareness of the importance of our past experiences as an influence in our current life has been present in the human consciousness from a long time ago.

In psychology and psychoanalysis the observation of the past is seen as an important way to understand what the person in the present is. In spite of the enormous differences between psychoanalysis and recapitulation, it is possible to see how the awareness of that past is destiny and is a constant in most people of the world.

In *Webster's New World College Dictionary,* the word *recapitulate* is defined as "to repeat briefly, as in an outline." Listed as a synonym is "repeat," which is a simple and clear approach to what the techniques of recapitulation are about. Repeating (in the sense of reliving) and summarizing (in terms of doing it in shorter time, looking for the basic structure) are actually part of the procedures that are the core of this book.

Developing Recapitulation Techniques

The work about the past, and even the idea of reliving the past as a step in a healing process, is present in many different therapeutic practices, from bioenergetics to hypnosis, from body therapy to orthodox psychoanalysis, and from primal therapy to the spiritual practices of different indigenous peoples. Nevertheless, the term *recapitulation*, associated with a systematic practice to heal ourselves from the damages obtained in the past, was introduced for the first time by Carlos Castaneda in his book *The Eagle's Gift** in 1982.

In that book Castaneda describes a very general procedure for recapitulation. Even though the theme is enticing, his description of the technique is too general, and what's more relevant for the readers interested in the practice is that his description does not provide the necessary background to apply those practices in the context of everyday life.

The idea of restoring the energetic body was very appealing to Castaneda's readers, but though the recapitulation practices described in his books were quite attractive, they were difficult to apply because of the enormous distance between the strange world described by the apprentice of the sorcerer and the life of Castaneda's readers.

As I have explained in my book *The Teachings of Don Carlos,* my relationship with the books of Castaneda was a little bit different from that of most of his readers, due to my connection with indigenous peoples

---

*Carlos Castaneda, *The Eagle's Gift* (New York: Simon and Schuster, Pocket Books, 1982).

who are inheritors of the ancient Toltecs' tradition.* My participation and
membership in the Toltec tradition gave me a much more practical understanding of those books. Having been trained in the *nimomashtic*† system, which is the rule in Toltec knowledge, it was natural for me to bring
into action every interesting practice mentioned in Castaneda's books and
to learn by myself.

This way, practicing by myself and then with the groups for personal
growth that I have coordinated for twenty years, I developed the modern
techniques that are the main content of this book. In its current way, these
practices incorporate procedures from the following:

- Procedures and adaptations of procedures that we learned among
  the Wirrarika people, whom I call the surviving Toltecs, which
  are related to the process of recapitulation, resulting in an em-
  powering of the whole process.
- Techniques that we have developed inspired in part by
  Castaneda's earlier books.
- Practices and modifications created by me and my teammates in
  response to the needs that appeared during the continual practice
  of recapitulation.

A few people have criticized our techniques, suggesting they are
not the same as those that Castaneda presented in his books. It is true
that our techniques are not the same as the ones presented by Castaneda,
and I am happy about that. Our goal has never been to imitate or blindly
follow Castaneda's writings but rather to develop practical and efficient
procedures in order to help people succeed in their own quest for healing, growth, and freedom. This work is more down-to-earth because it

---

*See *Toltecs of the New Millennium* by Victor Sanchez (Santa Fe, N. Mex.: Bear & Company,
1996).

†*Nimomashtic* is a Nahuatl word that means "teaching yourself." Nahuatl was the language spoken by the Toltecs; it is still spoken today by many indigenous peoples of Mexico.

is oriented to the people who live in this world and not in the so-called sorcerer's world.

The proposals presented in this work are the result of thirteen years of research—designing procedures, creating exercises, making mistakes and learning from them, and applying and testing the results with more than two thousand practitioners. This research has been public, open to anyone interested in participating.

We have had the participation of psychiatrists, psychologists, and psychoanalysts who have found our procedures highly effective as powerful tools for personal growth and transformation. Many of them are including parts of our procedures in their professional practices with their own patients.

For the first time, ways to connect the shamanic experience with the field of psychology and other sciences for health are being opened, and AVP is contributing to this process.

AVP: *El Arte de Vivir a Proposito*

The Art of Living Purposefully (AVP for its initials in Spanish*) is an organization that for twenty years has been working to bring to modern society the hidden treasures of indigenous knowledge. Due to its deep connection with the descendants of the historic Toltecs, AVP has adopted a second name: the New Toltequity. With this name, we are assuming our role in the tremendous task of rescuing and translating the Toltec knowledge so it can be understood and used by nonindigenous people. As I have explained in *Toltecs of the New Millennium*, it is my vision and belief that in the indigenous world—and in the surviving Toltecs' world in particular—there are responses to the most urgent problems in our modern societies.

Finally, the ultimate reason to open this work to the world is that we have lived in our own lives, and seen in many other people's lives, the

---

El arte de vivir a proposito.

positive results obtained by practicing recapitulation. This is not a story that was born in somebody's imagination. It is not something that I have heard or read, or that has been told by someone else. We have done it and the results are power, beauty, and freedom.

Are you ready to join us?

2

What Is Recapitulation?

Definition

Providing a definition of *recapitulation* is not difficult at all. The point here is that we are dealing with something that is beyond the boundaries of the rational mind—definitions cannot contain something so changing as the process of recapitulation. That is why many definitions for recapitulation will be provided throughout this work. Each of them will help you reach a deeper understanding of the process. Let's start.

Basically, recapitulation is what our energetic body does in order to heal itself from the damage incurred in the past as a consequence of negative energetic interaction.

To understand this, it is necessary to open our vision to the meaning of our existence as fields of energy—a completely different vision of ourselves from the one we have in the everyday world. According to Toltec knowledge, trying to understand our existence from the point of view of our ego and the rational mind results in a mostly confusing exercise where conflict between thought A and thought B is irresoluble.

The Toltec knowledge offers a much deeper and practical approach to our true nature: *We are the children of the Sun,** which in terms of energy means we are fields of energy. According to this vision, everything that happens to all the beings in the universe is related to their level of energy and to the kind of energetic interactions they have with the beings surrounding them. Humans are not the exception.

The Energetic Body

When we talk about the energetic body, we are talking about something that is different from the ego. It is different from that perception of ourselves as something that is located inside our head. It is even different from the physical body itself. The energetic body is bigger than our physical body, which means that it includes parts that we normally do not see, such as the energy surrounding the physical body, which is known as the aura; feelings; and the dreaming body. Ultimately, the energetic body is the one that feels, the one that connects itself with what is out there. It is the counterpart to the ego, which is basically connected to itself.

The energetic body is the biggest of mysteries. It is not possible to determine where it starts and where it ends. We may live part of its endless possibilities, but we cannot deplete them. It is because of our energetic body that we are simply another mystery in the middle of all the mystery surrounding us. We have no bottom.

To understand recapitulation it is necessary to talk about the energetic body. Recapitulation is done by the energetic body, which includes our physical body but is more than just that. The ultimate nature of all human interactions is that they are exchanges of energy—positive exchanges, negative exchanges, neutral exchanges, but exchanges in one way or another.

These exchanges lead to consequences. At the present, we are basically the result of those exchanges. Energetic exchanges were printed in our energetic body, and we live the way we live, we see the world we see, and we are what we are because of those exchanges and their energetic prints.

*See *Toltecs of the New Millennium*, by Victor Sanchez.

I know that at this point this explanation is too abstract, mainly because we do not see how the energy is being moved and affected by our actions and interactions. Nevertheless, as we advance in our presentation, the abstract will become concrete, and you will understand how those energetic exchanges and their results have been and continue to be experienced in your everyday life.

From now on, every time I mention the "body," please remember that I am talking about the *energetic body* and not the physical body. When I am talking about the physical body, I will specify this by calling it the physical body. Now with this in mind we can go ahead with our definition of recapitulation:

Recapitulation is the natural process of energetic restoration of our energetic body from the damages that come from the past. This natural act is done by our body. It consists of bodily remembering and reliving the meaningful events of our lives in order to perform a healing process to recover the state of energetic completeness and balance that we had when we were born.

Let us look part by part at the contents of our definition.

Natural Self-Healing Process

Recapitulation is a natural process of energetic restoration of our energetic body. This means that the energetic body heals itself. I can imagine many people's expressions of surprise at this.

"What are you talking about? A natural self-healing process that my body knows? I'm just hearing about this stuff recapitulation for the first time—and you're telling me that I already know how to do it? What are you talking about?"

I know it sounds strange, but the fact is, yes, we already know how to recapitulate and accomplish that process of energetic self-healing. To be more precise, I should say that it is our energetic body that knows how to recapitulate, which is different from saying that our personal ego or rational mind knows how to recapitulate.

The problem is that we are focused on our own ego most of the time, remaining far from our energetic body. In this way we block many of our natural self-healing processes, such as recapitulation.

Ego vs. Energetic Body

By always staying in the ego, we do not even know that there is more to what we are. Actually, we are not that ego. We are a field of energy. While the ego is an illusion or, more exactly, a spell, the energetic body is much more real. Actually, it is what happens to our energetic body that determines our destiny, and not all those explanations that our ego provides about itself through our talking mind.

To be focused always on our ego and thinking we are that ego is not something concomitant to human existence. We have been trained by our culture to believe that all behaviors, routines, and repetitive reactive ways of thinking about everything, including ourselves, is what we are. We think we are everything that is implied by the words *I, me,* and *self.* The ego is no more than a very detailed description of what we think we are, according to our personal history. It seems so real and so definitive because we have learned during our entire life to live as if the ego were the most real thing in this world. We are always acting in accordance with our ego, and by doing so we are reinforcing the perception that our ego is real. By reinforcing the conviction that we are just that—the ego—we reinforce acting in accordance with the ego, and on it goes, endlessly. This is how we become trapped in a vicious circle that is not easy to break.

 The not-doings,* or actions liberated by the process of recapitulation, are meant to break that vicious circle. Practicing the not-doings of the personal self can drastically prove the unreality of the ego. When we stop

---

*For a detailed explanation of the not-doings as used by the author, see *The Teachings of Don Carlos,* by Victor Sanchez.

acting in accordance with our personal history and the dictations of the ego, the ego scrambles, and we can see that we are not that ego. We can see, for the first time, how it is to be free.

These comments on the ego are relevant to emphasize the fact that focusing on the ego and believing that our self determines what we are is not the only way we can live. (Humanity has not lived in that jail for all time.) It has been the curse of Western society since the Greeks, when reason was placed on the throne as the best tool for human progress and knowledge. Peoples of ancient times and indigenous peoples of the present have chosen different ways, and that is why we have so much to learn from them. They have not separated themselves from the silent knowledge, the knowledge of the energetic body, as we have done.

Our Dual Nature

By denying everything that is outside the boundaries of the rational mind, modern humans have denied half of themselves. The indigenous Toltec people of Mexico did not make that mistake. They knew that we are double beings. They knew about the double nature of the world. That is why they call the world *Omeyocan,* or "the place of duality." That is why they give a name for each side of the world, and for each side of the duality we are: they named our rational side *tonal,* and our mysterious side *nagual,* the side of the silent knowledge. I am not talking about those invented Toltecs supposedly emerging from Atlantis or from another galaxy. I am talking about our great-grandparents, the ones who inhabited Tula in central Mexico, the ones who left us their architecture, their poetry, and their tradition to remember the path to our true nature.

Those ancient Toltecs were aware of our dual nature and envisioned the integration of the two sides of our being as the goal of human existence. Unlike the Aztecs, whose military vision of the world is represented in the shield of the Mexican flag featuring an eagle devouring a serpent, the Toltecs envisioned the two sides of the duality as the promise of integration represented in the flight of Quetzalcoatl, the feathered serpent. In the Toltec vision the eagle does not kill the serpent. The two creatures become one in the rebirth of a new being: the plumed serpent.(That was the dream of the ancient Toltecs, and that is the dream of the new Toltecs.)

With the awareness of our dual nature, we can understand better what has happened to us as members of the modern Western culture. We have lost contact and even the awareness of our magical side. In forgetting this, we have lost the source of our power. Without knowing, we have abandoned the experience of self-healing that was our natural inheritance in the times when humanity did not run away from the silent knowledge. The result is more and more disease. The more we create medicines for the benefit of the pharmaceutical industry, the more new diseases appear. Our natural mechanisms of self-healing are debilitated. The natural capacity to recapitulate and heal ourselves from the damaging experiences of the past is one of those precious treasures we have lost. That is the bad news.

The good news is that we can recover on purpose that capacity, which implies that not everything is lost. Now what we said before is understandable; our energetic body already knows how to do recapitulation while our rational mind does not know. Because our energetic body is able to perform the self-healing process, the way to fully heal ourselves lies in finding out how to go back to the awareness of the energetic body. And that is exactly what we do with the exercises for recapitulation.

Now that we understand that recapitulation is a natural process of self-healing, let us focus on the next part of our definition:

> It consists of bodily remembering and reliving the meaningful events of our lives in order to perform a healing process to recover the state of energetic completeness and balance that we had when we were born.

Ordinary Memory and Body Memory

The process of recapitulation involves the remembering of past events. But this remembering is not like the normal, mental recalling we continuously engage in during everyday life. While normal memory is basically *thinking,* body memory is closer to *feeling.* It is a process of reliving, which in one way is like going back to restore what was wrong. This does not mean that we can change the past. What we can change are the consequences that result from the past and the way these consequences are affecting our present life.

Actually, normal memory and recapitulation are so different that they each give us a completely different report of what our life has been. This is one of the reasons to call the memories that we get through recapitulation "the memories of the other self," or "the not-doing of memory."

Normal memory is a speech we have been telling ourselves throughout our whole life. It is the interpretation and the explanation we have been giving ourselves and others about what has happened in our life. Without being aware, those explanations have been changing all the time to suit the need or affirmation of our ego. That is the function of our normal memory—to support and justify what we are in terms of ego. While normal memories sustain the ego, recapitulation memories reveal the energetic body.

In fact, what I have seen again and again in our recapitulation workshops is people discovering that what they thought was their past was not real at all. What they used to call "my past" was no more than their own myth of origin.

Our Myth of Origin

The myth of origin of the ego (that thing which we call *me* or *I*) is the story we have unconsciously created to justify the way we are. That is why we are so attached to what we call our past. Even if it was terrible we secretly love our past and are very resistant to leaving it behind because it is what sustains our ego.

When we finally face our real past, it can lead to surprising discoveries: perhaps you learn you are not the victim but the victimizer. Or maybe, after a life pretending you have always cared about somebody or something, you discover while recapitulating that you have not cared at all about that person or situation. The opposite is also common. Perhaps you spent your life pretending you did not love or care for your father, only to discover at the moment of his death or through recapitulation that you have always deeply loved him.

One of the clearest examples I have seen of this is that of a man who has become one of my best friends. This is a true story, but I will change my friend's name to preserve his privacy.

Years ago Juan Carlos started as a participant in my workshops. He was very shy and silent. When he tried to talk to others, he stammered. Eventually he reached a moment when he was feeling more confident with his group companions and confessed what was hurting him. "I am thirty years old, and I have never kissed a woman!" he said. "I don't know how it feels. I am a thirty-year-old man, and I have never had a girlfriend. That's what hurts me. I don't want to be alone, but I don't know how to approach other people, especially women. I would like to be as any other man," he continued, "but that's my pain. I don't know how."

Everybody in the room was shocked. Juan Carlos was so normal. He was a slim young man, not a monster or anything like that. He had a profession and a good income. Then why was he sunk in that deep hole?

"But how is this possible? What happened to you?" the group asked.

Then he told the story of his life.

He had been a sad child because his father never wanted to play with him. To make matters worse, the other kids in his neighborhood rejected him because they thought he was strange, so he wasn't able to play with them either. What could be sadder than a child who does not play?

"I think that's why I grew up as a lonely, sad man," Juan Carlos said. "If my own father didn't want to play with me, what can I expect from other people?"

No one in the room said a word; everybody could feel what he felt. He was right. After we had listened to his terrible experiences, his current situation was understandable.

Juan Carlos continued with his work until the time when he started recapitulation. He was participating with fifty-six other women and men in our yearly fifteen-night intensive workshop of recapitulation. In that experience, the participants spent each night for two weeks inside a box for recapitulation. At the end of the first week, the night was especially intense. Movement and noise could be heard coming from the boxes; sounds of voices, screams, laughter, and singing were all mixed together. Participants were reliving intensely. Then from Juan Carlos's box we could hear a very loud shouting. We did not know what was going on, but we could feel that, whatever it was, it was very intense.

Later on, around 3:00 A.M., Juan Carlos came out of his box. He was screaming and laughing all at once. It was very strange; I felt a bit worried about his state. Then I could see that he was crying from happiness.

"It was a lie!" Juan Carlos was crying. "It was a lie!"

"What was a lie, Juan Carlos? What are you talking about?" I asked.

"My life! It was a lie!" he kept repeating. "It wasn't true. It wasn't true that my father never played with me!" While saying this, Juan Carlos kept laughing and crying at the same time, in a state of uncontrolled internal turmoil.

"I could remember playing with my father! He was in fact a worried and strict man, but he had made many good gestures of companionship—we played together!

"I could remember laughing! It wasn't true that I never played with other children. Memories came to me of the fun I had with other kids. It was a lie! Why had I lost my joy? It wasn't true. I am a normal man! How could I forget all that? How could I?" were the amazed questions of our friend.

Juan Carlos was happy to the point of tears for having recovered his joy and the love of his father. The story of the sad boy who then became a sad man was a lie that his ego used to avoid the risk of change.

Though it was a very happy night for Juan Carlos, and for all of us having the luck of sharing his time to awaken, the story did not end there.

Less than a month after the workshop, Juan Carlos solved his problem of not having kissed a woman. Certainly, he did a lot more than that. . . . Within a few months, he became a popular man among females. It got to the point where we had to warn him, "Slow down, man! You are not supposed to have everything you like!"

The story of Juan Carlos is just an example of how we are tied to a past that most of the time is just the fiction that we have built to justify our fear of change and negligence of attempts at changing. But his history is also an example of how powerful and healing the task of recapitulation is to our lives.

As we have seen, our ordinary memory does not give us a real report of what our life has been. That is the story of the ego. The real story of what we are is the story of our energetic body. When your energetic body tells its story, what you see is very different from the ego's version—it is not based on the ego's interpretation of what was pleasant or unpleasant, but is founded on what we and others have done to our energetic body and the subsequent benefits or wounds we have received. This story, despite the fact that it determines our entire life, is often forgotten, erased from normal memory—and it requires some work to recover it.

The important part is that through the act of remembering, our energetic body is able to take our awareness back to the event, so that we have a second chance to face the situation in a different manner. This process will be explained in detail later in this book.

Because recapitulation is a natural act, once we take our body to a specific situation and event, it should take control and do the recapitulation by itself. Unfortunately, that is not usually what happens. Let us see why.

In our everyday life, our body is not performing recapitulation by itself so we can heal and restore our energetic body in a natural way. This is because we are blocking the natural self-healing process by our persistence in protecting the ego and its demands.

Black Holes in the Energetic Body

If we get a scratch on our skin and our finger bleeds, the physical body will immediately react to generate a procedure of self-healing that allows the wound to close soon. Even with major injuries, our body always does its best to heal itself. But what would happen if we continually contaminate the wound, again and again? The wound would not close and would become a major problem to our system.

Yet that is exactly what we do to the damages inflicted on our energetic body: Because of our devotion to the defense of the ego at all times, our energy-wasting routines block the natural process of self-healing, making the damages or holes in our field of energy permanent. This is why we should undertake the challenge of recapitulating on purpose, through a complex and sophisticated series of techniques.

There is a very good example of how our energetic body is able to self-heal as long as we do not hinder the natural process: having children. When we have children we are giving a large amount of our own energy for the new being that is coming into the world. We actually achieve an energetic whole because of that.

Warriors Do Have Babies

The issue of warriors having children has confused some of Castaneda's readers. The confusion has to do with parts of *The Second Ring of Power** and *The Eagle's Gift*† where he introduces this idea of warriors choosing not to have babies in order to keep their energetic bodies intact. This gives

---

*Carlos Castaneda, *The Second Ring of Power*, Touchstone edition (New York: Simon and Schuster, 1979).

†————, *The Eagle's Gift*.

us the impression that warriors do not have children or that if we have children we are lost, and the warrior's way will never be for us. We could even go to the extreme: If everybody follows these ideas, this way of thinking would ultimately mean the end of humanity.

This is similar to the idea expressed in Castaneda's associate Taisha Abelar's book *The Sorcerers' Crossing,** where we find the statement that every time women have sexual intercourse, they are condemned for seven years to give their energy to the man they have had sex with, through the wormlike energy lines that the man leaves in the woman's womb.† Ergo, having sex is always wrong for women; celibacy is their only gate of escape. If you are a woman who has sex, you are lost. . . . Wait a minute! Are we talking about the teachings of shamanism or the churchlike morality of the Middle Ages?

These kinds of ideas could be very confusing. But this is the moment to remember that books are just books, and a better way to use them is to read them without abandoning the use of our own discernment. This means that no matter how much we love or like an author's work, it will always be okay to disagree with some parts of what we read. I know this sounds obvious, but the truth is that many readers do not dare to disagree with an author whose work they love because they feel that doing so would be akin to betraying their beloved author.

I do not think this is betrayal. On the contrary, my view is that serious authors are looking not for fanatics but for responsible readers who are going to read with attention what we write, then apply their own criteria to accept and choose what is useful for them and discard what is not. Looking for noncritical acceptance of everything we write would be the equivalent of building a cult to control and taking advantage of the followers' blind belief in us.

---

*Taisha Abelar, *The Sorcerers' Crossing,* Arkana edition (New York: Penguin Books, 1992).
†Ibid., 52–55.

To illustrate this point, I have found some deeply touching passages in Castaneda's books, such as the one in which don Genaro embraces the earth in a rapture of passionate love for the being that gives us home, nourishment, and destiny.* I felt touched to tears when I read this passage. While those emotions of joy and deep understanding are in my heart, they do not prevent me from saying that I consider aberrant the idea that having sex and having children is always wrong. I am myself a father, and I am very happy about that.

Nature as a Teacher

We can be confused by bizarre proposals such as the ones we have mentioned above when we stop seeing the natural world for too long a time. We become trapped in the enticing game of diving into more and more sophisticated mental explanations, however odd the ideas, that drive us to believe we are getting really deep knowledge. We come to a moment when we lose ground and we are flying in the imagination without being able to distinguish what is real and what is fantasy.

Instead of getting lost in so much thinking about bizarre ideas, we should close the book for a while; we should silence the talking to look around and see the way nature moves and grows and take advice from that. See the trees, the birds, the wind, and the miracle of creation. The Great Spirit would not have given us the impulse of love and procreation, as it did the rest of the living creatures, just for our condemnation. We do not need to be geniuses to understand that. We just need to think less and see more.

In the case of procreation, giving part of our own being for the existence of our sons and daughters is natural. Did we not receive energy from our parents? Did we not receive from the earth and the sun the energy

*Carlos Castaneda, *Tales of Power* (New York: Pocket Books, 1992).

and matter that our body is made of? Why then should we be so selfish as to deny giving up part of what we are for the re-creation of life?

Moreover, the hole that comes with having children is not supposed to be permanent. The natural process requires that we have that hole open in our luminous body for a while, until it gradually closes as part of the natural recovery process of our energetic body. It happens in the same way with a physical wound: Our physical body works to close it. Our energetic body tries to do the same with our wounds of love.

The problem again is that because of our bad energetic habits, such as spending our entire life trying to protect the ego instead of trying to take care of our energy, we block the process of natural self-healing—this is why after having children, most people lose their shine (On the contrary, if we learn to be more careful in the way we use our energy (life force) so we may keep or even increase it, we may certainly pass through the challenging and nourishing experience of being parents without losing our power.)

The most incredible point regarding recapitulation is that despite the fact that we block our natural process of self-healing, there are moments in everyone's life when our body performs recapitulation spontaneously.

The most dramatic of these cases is at the moment of death.

The Last Recapitulation

It is not possible to say why, but the very last thing all humans do at the end of their lives is recapitulate. People who have had near-death experiences report as one of the most common elements of the process the reliving of the most meaningful moments of their lives. It is a fact that people who accompany a relative at the last moment before death report that the dying person whispered words about situations from childhood, adolescence, or other periods of his or her life.

After this process of seeing their lives pass before their eyes, many people share in words their feeling of exquisite peace. The recapitulation puts everything in balance; all the luminous filaments of the field of energy are arranged to become pure consciousness, which means that everybody may die, in the very last moment, in peace.

Certainly, the moralist that we all keep inside could find this idea disturbing—the chance for every human being to die in peace regardless of the kind of life he or she led. But that is what happens, and nobody knows why.

The universe is a strange place. It is full of phenomena whose explanations do not fit in our head. Maybe we should finally accept it: Not everything that exists was born and developed in such a way that our rational mind can explain it. That is what the Toltecs did—they used their rational minds to create knowledge, science, and tools for their well-being, but they also respected the experience of living with the left side of their consciousness (the nagual awareness), which at the same time was incomprehensible to their right side (tonal, the rational mind). They were not offended by the presence of mystery; they learned to love mystery as an integral part of their lives.

The relevance of this is not only that we may see recapitulation as a natural process of the energetic body. By recapitulating our field of energy we also become balanced and our awareness is open to a higher level. Why should we wait to die to accomplish this process? It makes a lot of sense to recapitulate to live better, not just to die.

Spontaneous Recapitulation

The spontaneous arising of recapitulation is not restricted to the moment of dying. It may also happen to anyone experiencing special circumstances, such as a nervous breakdown, extreme periods of fasting, long periods without sleep, a deep physical massage, even a physical trauma.

Working with so many people for so many years, I have had the opportunity to see people enter into deep states of spontaneous recapitulation on several occasions. Once, a very serious businessman fell down on the ground, crying like a newborn baby and adopting the physical position of a baby in the womb during the practice of a simple physical, sportlike exercise. His wife was there, participating in the workshop as well. The man was a forceful kind of person and he knew it. Everybody agreed that he was strong. His wife, on the contrary, was humble and shy. Everybody thought she was the soft, weak half of the couple. Working with our entire body in nature gives us extraordinary chances to see what we are that we are not normally able to see. Something special happened in that workshop. The important man had such a weak physical body that he was reduced to the state of a defenseless child. He was clumsy and fearful. His wife, on the other hand, was strong and happy.

My view was that the ego of the man collapsed under the pressure of seeing the lie of his life: He was weak and the woman was strong, even though he always managed the situation to control her all the time. But this time was different—under circumstances beyond his control the truth arose and his ego collapsed. Once that happened, his energetic body took over, trying to enter into the healing process of recapitulation.

Certainly that was not the moment to stop the workshop and set the conditions so he could continue recapitulating right there. Actually, he was very scared, thinking that something terrible was happening. He wanted to go back to normality as soon as possible. So I helped him by talking to him softly, gently moving his body and teaching him a special way of breathing so he could recover control of himself. Later on I explained my view of the situation and encouraged him to accomplish recapitulation as soon as he could. I don't know if he did that. I doubt it.

On another occasion I saw a woman entering into spontaneous recapitulation because of a small blow to her body as a consequence of falling to the ground during a physical activity. She did not hurt herself at all, but her emotional state made her cry intensely without knowing why she was so sad.

Other times people enter into those states simply by passing through a certain place, smelling a certain scent, or hearing specific music. The spontaneous entering of the recapitulation process can be superficial or very deep, depending on the circumstances. When it happens, our rational mind is confused and scared and doesn't know what to do. We try to escape and go back to normality by talking to others, watching TV, or pursuing whatever feels usual. And that is what we do: we escape without knowing that our energetic body was trying to do something good and even necessary for our well-being. Unfortunately, usually we miss the message and never complete the process.

The Psychoanalysis Connection?

To close this chapter I want to add a comment about a question that very often arises in my recapitulation workshops when I am introducing the theme: Is recapitulation similar to what I do in sessions with my psychoanalyst or therapist?

It is clear that psychoanalysis deals with the patient's past. In this sense it could share similarities with recapitulation. At the same time, there are many differences.

The process of psychoanalysis is based on the mind and on the expressions of the ego. It is related primarily to words. The result is that after years in therapy most people remain the same, with the only difference being that now they are able to provide complex explanations of why they are the way they are. The main problem with psychoanalysis is that it does not take into account the dual nature of human beings. It is not possible to heal a double being just by attending to one side of his or her duality.

In recapitulation, on the other hand, the process is based in the energetic body. It is related to feeling and reliving, more than to thinking or analyzing. The result is that people can make extraordinary changes in their life in a very short period of time.

In the early years of my research on recapitulation, I considered it a left-side consciousness process *only*, not related to the rational mind. It was as if Western therapy was dealing with healing from the rational mind while recapitulation was done from left-side awareness. That is what I thought at the time I wrote about recapitulation in my first book. As will be clear in the following chapters, that vision was wrong. It took some years for us to discover it, but we finally did: Recapitulation is a process that involves the totality of the dual being, tonal and nagual.

Finally, I should add that I have many friends and associates from the fields of psychiatry, psychology, and psychoanalysis, and we have friendly discussions about the possibilities and limitations of each one's field of work. Some of them have even tried to equate the nagual with the unconscious. They are my friends, but I should say that trying to equate the unconscious with the nagual is simply pretending that the rational mind can explain what cannot be articulated with words. Anyway, arguing about concepts and ideas has never been a problem among us, because our continual focus on practice takes us to the place of actions and results, and that is clear to all of us.

My comments about psychoanalysis are related more to "orthodox" psychoanalysis and not to all the new currents appearing everywhere. The truth is that as the years go by, more and more psychoanalysts, psychiatrists, and psychologists are moving toward a more open and integral approach to the human being. Many of them are interested in shamanism, and certainly many of them are transforming and enriching their professional practice with elements of alternative ways of working, as is AVP and the New Toltequity. These professionals get their degree from the university, nicely locate it on the wall of their office, close the door, and then open the doors of mystery and explore these alternatives that were not included in their academic studies.

This is how many of the new practices for healing have been arising—from the vision of Carl Gustav Jung to transpersonal psychology, from the inclusion of Buddhism in the curricula of Western universities to Gestalt therapy. Even what is associated with spirit and magic is nowadays a field of interest for open-minded Western researchers in the field of health. The walls between science and magic are falling down. Maybe the future is not that far away when we will finally understand our nature as double beings. Maybe then science and technology could receive the necessary balance from the silent knowledge. Maybe then we may rise to a science and a technology like those of the Toltecs in their own time and place—ones that do not destroy life.

At the bottom line what counts are the results. And to that I can only add what one of my friends, a very famous psychiatrist, once told me after participating in one of our workshops in recapitulation: "I am amazed. I have been under psychoanalytic therapy for seventeen years. It has been a good support for my practice as a psychiatrist. But I should admit that in two months practicing recapitulation I have been able to change my life much more than in my seventeen years of psychoanalysis."

He was right.

3

What Can We Get from Recapitulation?

Now that we have a general vision of what this strange concept called recapitulation is, here is the moment to see why we should make a space in our everyday routines to enroll in such a peculiar process. What is the main goal of recapitulation? What can we expect? What are the results for those engaging in recapitulation?

The main goal of recapitulation is to restore the field of energy from the damage that it has received in the past through interaction with other fields of energy.

How does that restoration take place?

Recovering Energy

The kind of experiences that we need to recapitulate the most could be understood as times when our field of energy was damaged because of a negative (antienergetic) interaction with another field of energy. The typical energy-wasting interactions are the emotional interactions with other people. Those kinds of exchanges cause damage in our energetic field that most of the time remains with us for the rest of our lives. What we feel is that we are losing a part of ourselves, and that is so painful that we have to forget in order to stop the pain. The paradox here is that while those events are the ones that have left greater damage in our energetic body, they are also the ones that we have erased from our normal memory. But while the right side of our awareness forgets, our energetic body does not. Recapitulation gives us a chance to enter into that secret memory.

In terms of energy, it could be said that those energetic traumas leave a black hole in our luminous body. We do not see the hole, but the external expression—the energy-wasting routines of our life—may be noticed by the silent watcher (the stalker). These routines are an internal script that determines our external doings. Many different actions or situations in our life could be the expression of a single internal routine, such as having had many partners but lived the same history with all of them.

Those exhausting repetitions are the black holes in our luminous body, and through them we lose our power, or life force.

This image makes it easier to understand what could be seen as the main benefit from doing recapitulation: recovering the energy that we have lost along the way. Recapitulation is our best chance to fill the black holes in our energetic body.

It is common during the recapitulation process that the recovering of energy is experienced as recovering a part of your self that you thought was dead and lost forever. Perhaps it is that part of your self that you did not even remember. Yes, we have to recapitulate to recover our childlike joy, our bravery, our curiosity for knowledge, our enthusiasm for life—to reclaim our magic and power.

When did you lose your capacity to trust another human being? When did you lose your daring to dive into the mystery that is surrender to the call of love? These terrible losses are often related to specific moments and events of our life, moments in which we did not find a better response to what was happening to us than to suspend forever a part of our own being.

Recapitulation is the path by which to pick up those parts of our selves that were left along the way.

Detaching Foreign Energy

Detaching somebody else's energy that is attached to our energetic body is one of the results of a thorough recapitulation. In the same way that part of our energy was lost in those emotional interactions, part of other people's energy was left in our luminous body, and we could still be carrying those pieces. That foreign energy is forcing us to be something that we are not and is an obstacle to our freedom.

Have you ever found yourself acting like someone else? Maybe your father? Have you discovered that some of your battles are not really yours, but are instead the battles of some important people in your life?

The intensity of other people's presence in our life may become printed on our energetic body. That was the case with the famous and successful M.D. who fought for long years to become a doctor and achieve a good reputation and a big income, only to discover in the third quarter of his life that he never had liked being a physician. It was his father's dream, his father's battle. He nearly walked all the way to the finish line of his life, only to discover his work was not his dream—but there was no way to go back and recover those thirty years spent in another person's battle. That is really dramatic. We have only one life—just a single chance in eternity to live the way our spirit demands.

Becoming Free of Energetic Hooks

Another way of seeing the benefits of recapitulation is to notice that we are hooked to many situations, events, places, and people of our past. Because of those situations, we cannot freely go ahead and accomplish our dreams. Our body remembers if we were defeated in a meaningful battle of our childhood, and because it has a footprint of that defeat, we are going to keep living the same way in all the meaningful battles of our life, facing the same defeat.

If you were disappointed because the first time you felt love and expressed it you were violently rejected, that shame and pain are going to follow you wherever you go, and you will avoid confessing your feelings again. If somebody fails you when you were expecting loyalty, your faith in the whole human race could be lost. Of course, this does not happen with every tiny problem we have. I am using these images so that you might have an idea of the kind of energetic hooks I am talking about. These hooks are forged for us in those special situations. Each one of us has his or her own personal experiences during which these hooks were made. Certainly, most of the time we have forgotten these events, removed them from our normal memory.

Now you are in the present. You want to do things, make changes in your life. You want to start new projects, try new relationships, but you find it is not that easy. Something stops you. All your invisible but strong connections to your past experiences are like a weight that does not let you move ahead. You are stuck in the past. For instance, you cannot see a new person with new eyes because you see in her or him the presence of that other person who made you suffer. Such hooks condemn us to repeat the same stories again and again. That is why we may say that recapitulation is a door to freedom. Once we release those hooks, we have the chance for personal change, choosing how we want to be and how we want to live.

Releasing Promises

One of the amazing things that we may face through recapitulating is the discovery that we have really been living two lives: the one that our normal memory reports and the one that our energetic memory reports. It is like having forgotten the major events of our life; therefore, what we remember is more like the dream that the ego has been dreaming about itself. This is possible because of our dual nature. Both sides of our existence always have been present, even though normally we have noticed the tonal, our rational side. Here we are dealing with one of the ways to claim the other side.

Some of the most extraordinary things that are hidden—most of the time lost—from our normal awareness are the "promises." I call promises those energetic commands that were issued by our entire being under circumstances of tremendous pressure. In a very simple outline, I could say that the promises take place when we are engaged in a difficult emotional interaction. Under the pressure of what is going on in that event, we promise not to do something anymore or we choose to act in a different way from that moment on.

Let's see an example. Mary was a little girl, five years old, full of happiness and love. The world for her was an endless opportunity of exploration and discovery. Her mother, Jane, loved Mary deeply, but she was not expressive in demonstrating her love to her daughter. Only on very few occasions did she embrace and kiss Mary. She was not a bad mother—it just happened that she herself did not have affectionate parents; therefore, she did not learn the physical expression of love between parents and their children.

Jane expressed her love for her daughter in the care she put into all the things related to Mary. Her clothes for school were always impeccable. Mary had a beautiful room full of light, pink blankets on her bed, all kinds of tender toys, and smiling little bears painted on the ceiling. It was clear that Jane had made her best effort to create a beautiful space especially for Mary.

Nevertheless, there was always that feeling in Mary of missing something. She could not explain what it was, but each time she saw her mother after school or when the time for going to sleep arrived, she felt that sensation of missing something.

The end of the school day was not a pleasant time for Mary. These were the moments when the children who had been missing their parents met with the parents who had been missing their children. For most of them these were moments of joy and times for expressions of love. For Mary it was different. When her mother arrived at the school and they met, instead of being lifted up in the air for an embrace, a kiss, and maybe— why not?—a spin in her mother's arms, what Mary got was:

"How was your day in school?"

"Fine, Mom."

With a serious expression on her face, her mother took Mary by the hand and said, "You should be careful when crossing the streets! Pay attention to how I do it."

"Yes, Mom."

Then, for the rest of the way home, she and her mother would walk together in silence. Mary wanted to talk, run, and play, but she was afraid of doing something wrong because the vigilant look in her mother's eyes seemed to say: I am watching you. Do not do anything wrong.

Sometimes while sleeping, she dreamed that her mother was going to look for her at school and when they met her mother embraced her with affection and kisses—just exactly as she had seen the mothers of her companions do at school when they went to pick up their kids.

Mary's days at home were nearly silent; she talk with her dolls or the frog in the garden fountain. Her interactions with her mother were brief and basic:

"Wash your hands for dinner."

"Remember to finish all your vegetables."

"Who left this doll on the stairs?"

Her father was different. When feeling alone, sometimes Mary used to close her eyes and remember her father. What a nice feeling when that tall tender giant lifted her onto his shoulders with his strong, warm arms. The world seemed so different from those heights! What beautiful music he made when he took her onto his lap, embraced her, and sang that funny song.

What a shame that he spent so little time with her!

Sam was an itinerant salesman. He worked for a tool factory, and his job was visiting stores, offering the tools of the company to possible buyers. He was number two in the group of salespeople in the company. Being a responsible father and husband, he worked overtime to increase his income so that Jane and Mary could enjoy comfort and security. His favorite time was when he had the unusual chance to play with his little princess. That didn't happen often, but the work—he thought—was his first duty to his family.

There was a time when Sam took longer than usual—three days, in fact—to return home from work. Jane thought that Sam might have been sent to another city with his truck full of tools, and Mary was missing her father so much!

"When is Daddy going to come back, Mom?"

"Soon, soon—don't worry."

"How many days is soon, Mom?"

"A few days, don't worry. Go play in the garden."

In the garden, Mary did not feel like playing. Instead, she thought and thought about her daddy. She kept looking toward the driveway, hoping to see his big truck pulling in.

Sam was completely drunk at the end of the bar in a dirty pub. This was not the Sam that everybody knew and respected. This was a sobbing ghost. In the middle of the fog of his stunned mind he was seeing again and again the same story, trying to get to a different ending each time he recounted it.

His workday had begun as usual. But upon arriving at the company he was told that the manager was waiting for him. When Sam entered the meeting room, he felt something strange in the air. The room was full of all the salespeople in the company. The man in the speaker's place was not old Ed, the manager and friend whom Sam had always known. Where was Ed? A young man with a stiff face said:

"This company has been sold to McGraw Tools Inc., a Holland Corporation. I'm Mr. Deveraven, and this is the list of the salespeople who are going to continue working here. If you don't hear your name, go to the cashier to receive the payment of your pending commissions. Sorry, gentlemen, but the company needs to decrease its personnel in a process of restructuring to fit with the current condition of the country's economy. Good morning, gentlemen!" The stiff-faced young man left.

Sam was shocked. What was going to happen to him? He produced sales; he surely would be on the list. Then Mr. Sullivan, the number one salesman in the company, went on stage with a paper in his hands.

"Oh, no!" thought Sam. "If Mr. Sullivan is with them, I'm lost!"

Robert Sullivan was the kind of person who always wanted to be number one, and he did not like competition. He had always tried to put obstacles in Sam's way so that Sam could not approach him in numbers of sales.

"Dear friends," Sullivan began, while looking at Sam with a malevolent smile on his face. "This is the list of the selected salespeople; I wish you luck!" Sam knew exactly what was going to happen. He was right— he was not on the list.

He left the room completely shocked and depressed. While he was walking down the stairs, his depression became anger. He headed to the new manager's office, but the secretary said that there were no meetings times available with Mr. Deveraven. That was too much! Sam reached Mr. Deveraven's office door and knocked furiously.

"You can't do this to me!" he shouted. "I've been working here for fourteen years! I've helped this company earn a lot of money!" The door would not open. The next thing that happened was an unequal fight between Sam and four agents of the security staff of the company. Sam ended up beaten in the street while the security agents were removing the tools from his truck. Anger, humiliation, and hatred of life—that was what Sam was feeling in that bar. His life was ruined, just like that!

The next day found Sam sleeping on a park bench. It was 1:00 P.M. Tired, defeated, and angry, he decided to go home.

Mary was sitting in the front yard, combing the hair of Lucy, her favorite red-haired doll. She was thinking about her daddy, unable to imagine the hell that he was passing through. She heard the familiar sound of her father's truck and felt a jolt of excitement and joy. "Daddy!" she said, running to the truck. All the love that she felt for her father was overflowing. Oh, she needed to hug him so much!

Sam opened the truck door. He was still very depressed, angry, and dizzy from the effects of the alcohol. He could barely see a form moving toward him. Mary reached her father and embraced his leg while he was struggling to find his way to the front door.

"Daddy, Daddy! Do you want to play with me? Look! I've given Lucy a new hairstyle. Look!"

"Shut up! Don't bother me now! Can't you see I have problems to deal with? Go away!" Sam said, at the same time violently pushing away the little girl.

Mary fell down in the wet grass. There was mud inside her mouth and all over her face. She cried while trying to wipe it off and watched her father go into the house. He didn't even turn back to look at her. She was broken inside.

Why? Why? What did I do to make Daddy stop loving me? I'm a bad girl! This feeling filled her little body. Then another a feeling came from the depths of her being. . . . *I will never let you know that I love you. Nobody is going to know what I feel!*

Mary's promise was not just an idea in her mind. There were no words—not even thoughts. It was a silent feeling, with no other feeling or thought competing with it. It was an energetic command.

Mary was sad, but some time later she was playing with her dolls again, alone. Her father found another job, but he would never be the same. Mary grew up to be a beautiful woman and eventually became a schoolteacher. She is thirty-four, and her life is normal.

But even though she is attractive, healthy, and successful in her field of work, she has never had luck with men. Nine serious relationships have finished in the same way: These men left because they felt she was too cold. She doesn't like that, but she can't help it. She has fallen in love deeply three times, but not even then was she able to really give herself up to the man she loved. "Do you love me? Do you love me?" each would ask her many times, but she never could answer, "Yes, I love you." It was not that she did not love each of these men; it was just that from the depths of her being something prevented her from confessing her feelings. She hates herself for not being able to tell what she feels. If a man touches her with love, she cannot respond. Her entire body becomes stiff and closed. She is a virgin at thirty-four, and she knows she has a problem.

She has been going to weekly therapy sessions. The therapist has asked her many times if she remembers having been sexually abused, but she doesn't have any memory of anything like that. She simply cannot explain what is wrong with her.

Mary's story is that of a promise. Under the pressure of an inexplicable pain, she promised never to express her feelings again. It was not a thought—it was a pure feeling in the absolute focus of the inner silence. That is what I call an *energetic command*—it cannot be discussed or changed; it can only be accomplished. Only a new energetic command can cancel an existing command, and that is what we do during the work of recapitulation: make new energetic commands, on purpose.

The situation that pushed Mary to make such a promise was so painful that the only relief she could find was in forgetting. The event with her father was erased from her normal memory, so she cannot find what happened to her. She forgot the promise, but her energetic body has not. Day after day, the energetic command has kept operating without Mary's awareness.

All of us have our own promises, for similar or very different issues. The promises of our lives are determining what we are and what we can and cannot do. They are behind those repetitions we cannot stop. These promises are a very good reason to engage yourself in the task of recapitulating your life, to finish with a hidden energetic command that could be restraining your power and well-being.

Saying Goodbye

To conclude with the presentation of the benefits that can be achieved through recapitulation, we should talk about the chance to energetically say goodbye.

Saying goodbye is related to one of the most common energetic problems people have in their luminous being: They are attached to a feeling of denial. They have lost somebody who was very important in their lives, but they never accepted that fact. They never said goodbye. People in such a situation live in a state of permanent anger and pain because they never accepted the reality they had to face. The workings of this are amazing.

A young boy loses his father at the age of ten. He does not cry during his father's funeral, but within him, in the deep place of silence, there is a total feeling: *No. This is not happening. You cannot go. I do not want it! It is not true! You cannot leave me!*

The anger and pain are beyond words. Outside, we see only a serious boy. He seems to feel nothing, and he thinks he feels nothing. The pain is somewhere else, not in his right-side awareness. He believes he is okay, but the turmoil and the pain have been sent to a much deeper place.

His life goes on, but he will never be the same. He is now a man, but his anger at and denial of his loss will always be there, hidden behind everything he does, stealing his chance of being happy every time something good happens to him. He may smile, even laugh, but never with complete laughter. He has an energetic knot deep inside. Maybe he doesn't notice it, but through the years his face has been marked by the scars of his anger, rarely disguised by an occasional gesture that tries to be a smile.

He doesn't know why sometimes he can feel a knot inside; he just does not make the connection. When he talks about his father, he says, "I don't know why everybody was crying. I was relaxed, playing around as usual. I felt nothing."

People in similar situations know they have never been the same since the loss of a dearly loved person. They just have never known how to overcome it.

Others are still losing energy because they never accepted the loss of a former partner. (The lovers were so attached that when one of them left he carried a part of the one who stayed.) Not being complete, the one who stayed will hold that pain forever.

Though the circumstances may be different, all the cases are the same: They are all people who are not able to say goodbye in the proper moment. Saying goodbye does not mean that you are not going to feel sadness or even pain for the loss of someone you love; it means that you feel the grief of the mourning for a period of time, and then you accept it and start to recover your well-being. Finally, one day, your mourning is finished. But in order to be healed, you need to accept it and say goodbye at a certain moment. Only then does the recovering start.

The recapitulation process provides a very good chance to go back to that time, that person, that denial and pain, to finally accept it and say goodbye. That is the time to see into that person's eyes, to feel the warmth of his or her presence and say: *My dear father* (or whoever he or she is), *I have loved you so much. I love you so much. You have loved me and given me so much joy with your love. I deeply thank you for that. Your time to leave arrived, and I did not respect that. Now I accept it and set you free to go wherever you should go. Your love will be always with me as a precious gift, and my love for you will be always part of my being. I give you back your freedom, and I recover mine. Goodbye.*

How many people need to pass through that healing process?

Be attentive, because it may be you.

4

How the Process of Recapitulation Works

Now we are getting to the final part of the background of recapitulation. This is the time to insert the final piece so that you can understand the entire process, from the moments when the energetic damage was done to the moment when you have healed your energetic body from those specific wounds.

This simple general understanding is fundamental to enabling the recapitulation practitioner to:

- Perceive the "thread" that unites all the steps of recapitulation
- Have a sense of the target of the recapitulation "thread"
- Achieve the personal general sense of purpose that is a fundamental element for a successful process of recapitulation

For an easy understanding of the damaging and healing process related to recapitulation, I have divided it into the following stages.

Average Life Sequence

	Energetic Body Process	Ordinary Reality Process
1	Energetic completeness	Newborn state
2	Antienergetic exchange	Intense emotional interaction
3	Energetic damage	Emotional wounds, promises, energy losses, etc.
4	Behavioral change	Repression, fear, emotional blocking, negativity, etc.
5	Damage reinforcement	Repeating behavior in any new situation
6	Increasing weakness	Loss of life force; tiredness, boredom, sickness, etc.
7	Death from exhaustion	Death in decrepit condition

This is the average person's life sequence—what normally happens if we do not do something about it. The new Toltec warrior's way, however, moves toward a different result, because by introducing recapitulation we change the last steps; we do not need to live feeling powerless and exhausted. This alternative sequence will be seen later in this chapter.

As we may see in the previous list, a noticeable external manifestation is associated with each stage in the energetic body status in accordance with our nature as dual beings. This means that although the energetic body is not perceived by our everyday awareness, the external expression of its status is easily noticeable if we simply choose to watch consciously. (It should be noted that these stages are presented here in a very general way and variations do occur.) Now let's look at an overview of each step, so we may relate it to our own experience.

Energetic Completeness

When a new human being is born, the energetic body is complete. There are no black spots, knots, or holes. All the filaments of the luminous field are in place, in perfect order and shining with the beauty of the first light. This is what I call energetic completeness. We all began this way. The war of the ego against the energetic body has not begun. Tonal is just beginning to be. We are all nagual; the world has no defined shape, and neither have we.

There are no restraints. If we feel, we express what we feel. There are no contradictory feelings inside. This is why little children are magical beings. Unlike the power of adults, their power has not been damaged from living internal fights within themselves. Have you noticed this? Have you noticed how often we adults are trapped between two opposite feelings at the same time? We want to look for a new job, but we are afraid of losing the one we have. We fall in love, but we cannot accept it for fear of being abandoned. We love our parents, but we hate them because they have not loved us enough. We want to start something new, but we are afraid to take risks. Being trapped under this torture with no way to go forward and no way to go back, our power is drained and we live without passion. Living without passion is living without power, and living without power means that we are giants living dwarves' lives.

With no contrary thoughts or contamination from fears and fantasies, children are powerful beings. They have the ability to concentrate their whole energy in a single action. That is called *intent.* For this reason they can see things adults don't, and they have answers for adults' problems that those who are grown are not even able to listen to. Children are wise, even if adults cannot see it. We are so obsessed with teaching them that we do not notice what masters they really are.

All this has to do with the fact that our energetic condition at the moment of birth is completeness. By interacting with adults, we start to lose part of our brilliance. The more we grow, the more we lose shine and become like them. Bear in mind that I am talking about a general tendency. Certainly there is a big difference in the process, depending on the energetic quality of the atmosphere and the people we grow among.

The following drawing is a representation of the energetic body at the moment of birth.

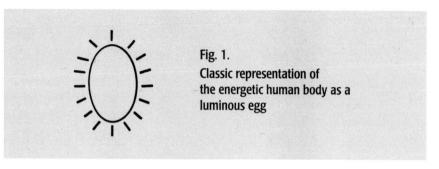

Fig. 1.
Classic representation of the energetic human body as a luminous egg

In the beginning of life our energetic body is like a piece of paper with nothing written on it. Unfortunately, that state of energetic well-being is destined to change.

Antienergetic Exchange

Interacting with other fields of energy (e.g., the people in our childhood world) produces changes in the energetic body. These exchanges could be of several varieties:

- *Energetic.* Those that are beneficial for keeping or increasing our level of energy
- *Antienergetic.* Those that diminish our level of energy
- *Neutral.* Those that do not affect our level of energy

To really understand the significance of this vision in our life, it is important to remember that our level of energy affects everything we do and everything that happens to us. Under the light of this vision, the two most extraordinary changes we may carry out in our life are:

1. Restoring the damages to our energetic body (recapitulation)
2. Changing the way we live to allow us to increase energetic actions while diminishing antienergetic ones; "living purposefully"

Since the subject of this book has to do with restoring the field of energy, we are going to focus for the moment on antienergetic interactions and exchanges, because they are the ones that have damaged the energetic body.

The following graphic is the representation of an antienergetic interaction between a child in a state of energetic completeness and her father, whose energetic body is damaged from the process of taking care of the ego's needs, instead of taking care of his energy. Do you remember Mary's story about how she was rejected by her father when she needed him? Let us say that this is the moment when Mary ran, full of love, to embrace him and her father violently pushed her away.

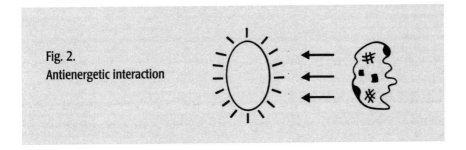

Fig. 2.
Antienergetic interaction

Energetic Damage

Now let's see the result of this for the formerly healthy luminous being.

Fig. 3.
Mary, right after the painful encounter
with her father

What do these illustrations mean? Figure 2 is the moment of the energetic trauma. Figure 3 represents the result of the trauma for the formerly healthy luminous being. Both illustrations represent what we do not see: that is, what is going on with who we are as fields of energy. (Because none of this can be seen, the mere idea of being fields of energy is strange for us.)

To the naked eye, what we are seeing in figure 2 is a five-year-old girl with an adult. She is full of love and wants to express her feelings; he is full of anger and pushes her away. There are two stories superimposed on the same event: the story of what is going on between two human beings and the story of the interaction between two fields of energy.

In figure 3 we see the result of the antienergetic exchange. The energetic body has a wound now. Energy is being drained through that wound. If there is no healing soon, the field of energy is going to get weaker as time goes by. In ordinary reality, what we would see in this stage is the little girl crying.

Behavioral Change

Now let us see what the internal process is for the person. Mary is emotionally shocked. Under the pressure of the pain and not being able to understand what is going on, she makes a silent energetic command (the promise): *I will never let others know what I feel!*

She has learned that expressing what she feels brings hurt. From now on she will be different. Before, she was able to express her feelings and establish contact with other human beings. After the painful event, she is not.

She starts hiding what she feels from her parents and relatives. She cries only when she is alone. Later on, during her teen years, the idea of confessing attraction or love to other adolescents terrifies her. A *doing* has been established. She has learned to hide her feelings; she does it again and again. She is not deciding this—she is suffering this, and she cannot stop. She just does not know how. Each time she acts like this she is losing energy through the tremendous stress that such a conflict produces in her. By repeating this internal routine (doing), she loses life power and is weakening more and more as time goes by.

Current Damage

Mary is thirty-four now. The following graphic shows the current condition of her field of energy.

Fig. 4.
Energy field condition of a human being after years of energy-wasting routines

Despite the not-nice appearance of this drawing, people in the ordinary reality do not see Mary as an ugly or sick woman. On the contrary, she is still a beautiful, strong, healthy woman. Because of the strength of youth, the wounds on her energetic body have not reached her physical body. Yet the damage is inside. She is unable to express her feelings. Because of this, her capacity to accept love from others is numb. To the men who "abandoned" her, she was an ice floe. One of them, Simon, really loved her, but he had to leave, convinced that Mary never loved him. The ironic fact is that she loved him dearly but was unable to express it.

Obviously, this is an oversimplification to provide a straightforward and clear understanding of how the damaging of the energetic body takes place, both from the perspective of the energy and the perspective of ordinary perception.

Regarding the traumas that are printed on our energetic body, it is important to notice the following:

Not all the antienergetic events of our life are destined to become permanent damage. Many times things do not go that far. To be congruent with our example, let us say that not all the children have a permanent wound as a consequence of any kind of rejection from their parents. Actually, under normal circumstances our energetic body is able to recover from minor injuries by itself. That is what happens when a child feels rejected because his mother does not want to play with him at a particular moment. He cries for a while, but in the next moment he is happily playing with his sister. At the level of the field of energy, this could be seen as a small scratch that heals naturally in a short period of time.

Our current condition is the result of the mixed effects of all the good things and all the bad things we have experienced that strengthen or weaken our energetic body.

Why, at times, do some people suffer deep damage in the energetic body by certain emotional interactions while others do not? What are the decisive factors for why in some circumstances we are able to overcome difficult situations while in others we are not?

The answer is a combination of the following factors:

- The energetic intensity of the event
- The way we react in relation to the event
- Whether or not we settle an internal routine (doing) as a consequence of the event

What I call the *energetic intensity* of the event is almost obvious. It is not the same to say to a child, "You cannot play now because it is time for homework," as it is to beat the child when he or she asks for a hug.

The way we react refers to the way we handled the situation in that moment. It is important to notice that our reaction is not the only one possible for that specific event. Did we react with hatred or with feelings of humiliation? Or maybe we found a way to explain or justify what was happening? Because of the way we felt did we overcome and let the bad experience pass right by, or did we make an energetic command that perhaps has ruined our life?

All three factors are connected. The same way our reaction relates to the intensity of the event and the internal resources we had at that moment, the settling of new routines has to do with whether or not we reacted by making an energetic command (for instance, "I will never be a winner" or "I will never let others know what I feel").

If we settle a new doing or internal routine that keeps the energetic wound bleeding forever, so to speak, it is a fact that the wound or hole in our energetic body is going to keep weakening us and endlessly taking away our power.

In summary, the way these three factors mentioned above come together determines which emotional interactions are going to result in permanent damage and which are not. Basically, without knowing, we have been living in the middle of a battle between our self-healing capacities and our energy-wasting habits. In most people's lives, the energy-wasting habits have the advantage.

It is very interesting to notice that the last two of those three factors are determined by each of us, and even the first one has quite a bit to do with us. This takes us to a major issue related to self-healing and reclaiming our power: *responsibility*.

Responsibility

Fear and self-pity (which is the other face of self-importance) are a very strong part of the psychological structure of many people in modern society. Because of this, one of the most common ideas related to our past and what we are is that we and the life we live are the result of what other people have done to us. We are full of sentences that express that kind of fantasy: that we fail because of what others have done to us.

"I am the way I am because my mother didn't love me enough" (hidden implication: "It is my mother's fault that I treat you like trash").

"I become angry and intolerant because my father was too strict and punished me too often" (hidden message: "Blame my father for my beating my children as if they were punching bags").

"If I had not been so alone when I was a child, I would have been a better student" (hidden message: "If I am a mediocre person, it is not my fault but my parents' fault").

Or the opposite: "I grew up with my grandma. She always overprotected me. She never let me do anything by myself. How can you develop with such treatment?" (hidden implication: It is not my fault for being an alcoholic and a loser; it is my grandma's fault").

In one way or another, there is always somebody else to blame for our flaws. That is why we are so attached to our past regardless of whether we think our past was great or terrible. It is the myth of origin of what we are. It is the justification of our ego.*

What I am describing is the vicious circle of the modern person. It is the vicious circle of most of us. In order to break free from that circle, we should be warriors fighting to go back to our sacred nature of light and live accordingly with that.

The first step to being a warrior is taking responsibility. Accepting responsibility for what you are and how you live is a prerequisite to change and to improving your life. Stop blaming others. Stop blaming the world. Stop blaming this modern society that is so far from the Great Spirit. You are responsible. Accept it right now. Just like that.

Warriors are so committed to being responsible for their lives that they automatically assume taking responsibility for their past. Nobody has ruined my life. It is I who have done it. Therefore, it is I who may heal it.

That is one of the main keys of recapitulation. That awareness of being responsible for what happened and for what is going to happen should transpire in all its steps and techniques.

I can imagine the kind of thoughts that may be coming to your mind regarding such proposals, because I have heard them in my seminars and workshops many times:

Q. Why should I take responsibility for my father's faults? He treated me like trash!

---

*It is important to notice that when I say, "It is the justification of our ego," instead of saying, "It is the justification of what we are," it is because I want to make a distinction between what we think we are (I call it *ego*) and what we really are—fields of energy. Opening to that deeper vision of ourselves as luminous beings instead of living under the fantasy of being *me* or *I* is one of the most hard-won and greatest victories we may have on our way to being what we really are.

A. You should not take responsibility for your father's actions. You should take responsibility for the way you react to his actions. You are not responsible for his treating you like trash, but you are responsible for feeling like your life is ruined and having lived as though it is.

I know it is not a nice thought; actually, it is disgusting to our sensitive ego, but it is necessary to face it and accept it if we really want to change. Listen. We cannot change the past in the sense that we cannot change the fact that certain actual events took place. But we can change the results from our past by recovering the energy and the parts of our selves that we left along the way. Even more, we can change the past in the sense of changing the feelings we have about the past.

Just remember the story of Juan Carlos told earlier. He used to have a terrible, lonely past. By taking responsibility and doing recapitulation, he has a happier past. As a consequence of this energetic change, he does not need to keep worshiping an ugly past by living an ugly life. He may choose how to live now.

Think of your own examples. Maybe your father gave you a strong slap just because you answered him in a rude manner: "Don't talk to me like that! (slap) You must respect me because I am your father!"

You never forgave him for that slap. You have grown, made an independent life, and tried to be happy. But that slap that you cannot forget still hurts you thirty years later. Now, who is responsible for that?

Let us say that your father was responsible for his irritability and for the twenty minutes of your physical pain as a consequence of the slap. But you are responsible for the other twenty-nine years, eleven months, thirty days, twenty-three hours, and forty minutes of painful resentment that you have kept in your heart. You have hoarded that slap and that pain like the most valuable treasure. That is what helps you to feel that you are you. Maybe your ego has been built on that feeling. Well, I am sorry to tell you that maybe you have been hoarding something worthless.

Q. I could agree with what you are saying if I think about something not so terrible, such as being slapped by your father. But what about something more extreme? What if you were the victim of sexual abuse and that is destroying your life? How can you apply taking responsibility in that case?

A. In an extreme case like this, it is very important to take responsibility to stop suffering. We all agree that being sexually abused is one of the most violent aggressions a human being may suffer. There is no arguing about that. The point here is this: Let us say that you survive that terrible experience. What do you do after having suffered the aggression? Are you going to leave the pain behind as soon as you can, or are you going to keep it within you for the rest of your life? Are you going to be the victim for the rest of your life and maybe use that to justify your negligence to change?

Let me give you an example that is even more extreme and show how taking responsibility makes all the difference in how negative circumstances are going to affect our lives.

What event can you think of that is more horrifying than the experience of the innocent victims in the concentration camps controlled by the Nazis? Let me tell you about a doctor who was taken to one of those places of terror and, under such extreme conditions, took responsibility for his life. He suffered terrible tortures, and his life had no value at all to his warders. His body was reduced to skin and bones. He became a phantom of himself. But instead of abandoning himself to self-pity, he used his terrible experience to make a priceless discovery.

He thought, "Well, here I am nothing. I have nothing. They are doing what they want with me. There is no way for me to resist. But there is one single thing they cannot take away from me: the right to decide how to react to what they are doing to me. I have the freedom to choose my internal reaction. They can take my life, but they cannot take the freedom of my spirit. As long as I stay alive, they are not going to defeat my spirit."

So he thought and so he did. While suffering life in the concentration camp, he started to study the reactions of both prisoners and warders in such extreme conditions. He used his time to learn about the one decisive factor that allows some human beings to keep their inner strength and balance under circumstances of extreme suffering while others break down.

"They can hurt my body and even kill me," he thought, "but they cannot take away my ultimate freedom: the power of choosing how to react to what they are doing to me." He was right. His name was Viktor Frankl, and while staying in the concentration camp he developed the basis of a revolutionary approach to psychotherapy known as logotherapy.*

Certainly, you may say yes or no to taking responsibility regarding what your life has been and what your life is going to be. It is up to you. But before you say yes or no, be aware that your decision regarding whether or not to take responsibility for your past life is going to make the big difference in the kind of life you are going to live for the rest of your existence.

Making the Difference

In the preceding pages, we have seen the sequence from the initial energetic damage to the current damage. We have observed how that sequence takes place, both at the level of the energetic body and at the level of ordinary reality. Now let's see what happens when we reach the decision to make the difference by doing recapitulation. This decision and the consequent movements are no less than the decision to change our destiny.

When we talk about fate, there is something handier than looking at the stars and planets to see what is waiting for us in the future: We can learn what may be in our future by looking to our past. The footprints of our past are printed on our energetic bodies. The holes, scratches, knots, and dark areas appear in ordinary reality as repetitive

*See Viktor Frankl, *Man's Search for Meaning* (New York: Washington Square Press, 1998).

energy-wasting actions. The internal routines that sustain the structure of the ego—those events of the past and their footprints—created the structure of our ego. We were not like that when we were born. We were born without name, without past, without story, without fears or desires. Those things appeared later, while we were growing up. During the past, that which we call *me** was formed, and that structure determines what we are and what we will be. In this sense we do have a destiny, which is nothing other than projecting our past into our future. The future is the projection of the routines created in our past, toward a time in which those routines are going to happen again and again, until the exhaustion of our life force.

By the way, it should be clear that those negative ways of using our energy are not all that we are. There are some or many positive ways of using our energy that may be taking place in our lives as well. Actually, the way we live is just the balance between our energetic and the antienergetic actions.

It is because one of the main purposes of recapitulation is to seal the black holes in the energetic body and to stop those draining energetic habits that while introducing this work emphasis is put on the antienergetic section of what we do. Furthermore, when we deal with the recapitulation techniques, we will see how important it is to include the "positive" events in the whole process.

Now let's see how the recapitulation process changes the sequence: energetic completeness—emotional interaction—initial damage—energy-wasting habits—current damage—weakening—dead from exhaustion.

It is between the stages of current damage and weakening that we get the chance and motivation to undertake recapitulation. It means *now*. Now is the moment to change our destiny by breaking free from the past through recapitulation. *now!!!*

---

*For a more detailed explanation of the ego as merely a description, see *The Teachings of Don Carlos,* by Victor Sanchez, chapter 5, "The Not-Doings of the Personal Self," 96–98 and 110–11.

Basically, the liberating process could be seen like this:

The New Toltecs' Alternative Sequence

	Energetic Body Process	Ordinary Reality Process
1	Energetic completeness	Newborn state
2	Antienergetic exchange	Intense emotional interaction
3	Energetic damage	Emotional wounds, promises, energy losses, etc.
4	Behavioral change	Repression, fear, emotional blocking, negativity, etc.
5	Damage reinforcement	Repeating behavior in any new situation
6	Increasing weakness	Loss of life force; tiredness, boredom, sickness, etc.
7	Energetic restoration	Recapitulation process
8	Behavioral change	Not-doings
9	Healing reinforcement	Living purposefully
10	Energetic completeness	Health, love, productivity, creativity, etc.
11	Dying as a warrior	Natural death in state of health and power

Notice that stages one through six are the same as the ones on the earlier list of stages in the life sequence for average people. We have studied those stages in the preceding pages.

At the moment you are reading this we are in stage six; we are in the ordinary process of weakening as a consequence of the energy-wasting routines coming from our personal history. But we want to change our destiny and we are not going to wait just to see ourselves grow weaker and weaker.

Therefore, stage seven on our list is doing recapitulation. Figure 5 shows the transition to this stage, representing recapitulation with the box, a very powerful tool that is used in the process.

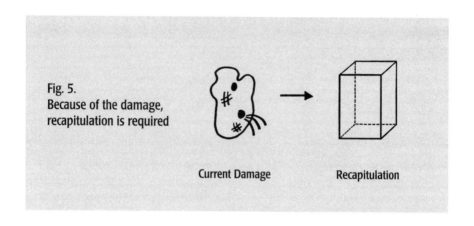

Fig. 5.
Because of the damage,
recapitulation is required

Current Damage   Recapitulation

The recapitulation techniques, as we will see in the following part of this book, heal the energetic body, sealing the black holes.

Here we arrive at one of the stages that provided the incentive for careful observation during our research. Ten years ago we believed that by doing recapitulation we achieved complete healing—the person could return to his or her life without having to face the same problems that were overcome by having recapitulated. That, we discovered, was not accurate. To our surprise, we found some of the practitioners going back to old energy-wasting routines within a period that varied from six to twenty-four months after recapitulation.

Even though this phenomenon was occurring with only some of those who had gone through the process of recapitulation, I was very worried. My statements about recapitulation in my first book did not take into account this possibility. Confused, I did what a Toltec does when he or she faces a mystery that may not be solved by ordinary means: I asked the Grandfather Fire.

Following the procedures that Toltecs and their ancestors have used throughout millennia, I asked the Fire what we were doing wrong. And the Fire gave us an answer, one that was connected to other anomalies we had found during the practice of recapitulation. In 1994, while having our yearly intensive workshop in recapitulation, something unusual happened.

We conduct this workshop in a big mountain lodge surrounded by woods in South Mexico City. There is no electricity service supplied to this place, but a generator is used to feed some lightbulbs.

In this workshop participants engage in some Toltec exercises before entering a box, and then spend the whole night doing recapitulation inside this box, with one break between 2:00 and 3:00 A.M. for another exercise. The work is finished around 6:30 A.M. I can imagine that this might sound very strange for those who are not familiar with the dynamics of such an experience. After looking at the practical parts, it will be seen that these kinds of procedures make more sense than they seem to at first glance.

During this particular workshop in 1994 we had reached the 2:00 to 3:00 A.M. break and were about to start an exercise when the generator failed and left us in darkness. The coordinators went to check out what was wrong with the generator after saying to the group, "Wait a few moments, please; we are going to see what is going on with the generator. Please stay quiet while we're gone." To our surprise, we returned after adding gas to the generator to find that the group was not respecting our direction at all. They were all talking about their experiences trying to recapitulate inside the box. At that time we were in the first days of the work, when the process is a little bit more difficult and the participants are like engines that are warming up, and have not yet taken off. In our absence they were having an intense conversation about the process.

"Wait a minute, wait a minute, what are you doing?" I said. "Haven't I told you many times that recapitulation is a left-side experience and that if we engage in right-side conversations we're going to land in the right side, making recapitulation harder to achieve? I'm afraid we're going to have problems tonight, because you have pulled your attention to the right side." I tried to refocus the group: "Remember, we should cross from the right-side awareness to the left-side awareness to enter into recapitulation. Okay, let's try to do the best we can. Next time remember my instructions."

The morning after, I discovered that something unexpected had happened. Everyone was very excited because the second segment within the box had been the most successful for them so far! I was amazed(That result contradicted the theory our practice was based on.)

The next night, I decided to conduct an experiment. During the 2:00 to 3:00 A.M. break, the group was asked to work in teams of five people each. What was the plan? To talk about their experiences, results, and obstacles in the recapitulation process—only this time on purpose. The results were amazing but consistent with those of the previous night: the process improved. What was going on? During the very same workshop the answer arrived.

One of the regular practices of our workshops in recapitulation is the work with the oldest and most powerful of the *poderios**: the Grandfather Fire. It was during one of those nights around the fire, when we were practicing *neneviery*†—opening our hearts and asking for advice. Then the vision came. I could see what had been wrong from the beginning.

One of the most impressive aspects of recapitulation is the experience of reliving past events. The box or whatever is around you disappears, and suddenly you are there reliving in the present what happened a long time ago. It is an entrance to a separate reality when time and space are not what they normally are.

Poderio is a Spanish word that is not common in the ordinary language. I have taken this word from the Wirrarika, indigenous people who keep alive the tradition of the ancient Toltecs. It means something similar to *power*, but it is not quite the same, because the Spanish translation of "power" is *poder*. *Poderio* means something closer to "special power," something like an entity or force that belongs to a specific place in the universe. There are *poderios* belonging to their sacred places in the desert or the mountains. There are *poderios* belonging to many places in nature, such as rivers, lakes, springs, and ravines. Then there are the five big *poderios* that rule the realm in which we live: Grandfather Fire, who is the oldest; the earth, who is our mother; the sun, who is our father and son of the Fire; the wind, who is our brother and also the messenger who communicates among all the *poderios;* and the water, who is also our mother.

† *Neneviery* is the offering to the Fire, consistent with talking in an intimate way to the Fire, with the words coming from the heart.

This is impossible to live with our ordinary right-side awareness. Entering into the space of recapitulation is entering into the "other side." Because of that, I made every possible effort to move away from the right side in order to achieve what we called a deep state of nonordinary reality named recapitulation. It seemed to be congruent, and it worked. Nevertheless, there was a problem. Something was missing—the right side.

That was the message of Grandfather Fire: We are double beings, tonal and nagual. Both sides are always present. Both were present when we passed through those difficult events that we need to recapitulate. Both need to be present to achieve healing!

Of course! We are double beings. We need to do the healing using both sides. That is why talking about the recapitulation was useful! Suddenly, everything started to fit into place. The puzzle began to make sense.

This was the first light for new discoveries in recapitulation. Later on, more and more pieces kept dropping into place. Seeing recapitulation as a left-side procedure was a mistake. We are double beings, and the healing should happen in a whole way, connecting the two sides. Each side has its own resources, and both should be used.

In the same way, we found a solution to the mystery of those recapitulation practitioners who, after completing their process, returned to old routines that were supposedly gone: When the initial damage was done, the two sides of our being were involved; therefore, to reinforce the healing both sides should be involved. Let us see.

First, we were part of an emotional interaction that took place in ordinary reality (right side); then we made an energetic command (left side); after this we block the natural healing process by introducing a new energy-wasting routine, or doing, which takes place in ordinary reality. Both sides are present. Furthermore, if it were not for the persistent practice of the doing, our energetic body would heal the energetic wound by itself.

Now in the same way that the doing in the right side was a requisite to reinforce and make permanent the initial damage to the field of energy that took place in the left side, the practice of the not-doing in the right *side is a requisite to make permanent the healing of the recapitulation in the left side.*

The secret lies in reversing the whole process. The following figures show how this is done. The practices of recapitulation produce a "provisional restoration." It is like putting on an "energetic patch" to seal the energetic wound.

Fig. 6.
Provisional restoration:
Recapitulation "patches" the energetic body

This is the moment when we have finished working with recapitulating the events from our list of events. We feel relieved and stronger, because we have stopped draining energy through the former holes in our energetic body. At this point, stopping energy-wasting routines is possible. We feel so happy that we may have the expectation that we are free from our personal history. But the process is not complete. In order to reinforce those energetic patches so they become permanent, we need to practice the purposeful acts of not-doings, which are congruent with the recapitulation process.

Liberated Acts

Now is the time to go back to Mary's story. Let us imagine that she gets to the point of deciding to undertake the challenge of recapitulation in order to heal herself of her problem.

She made the list of events and accomplished the work in the wooden box. She found that event when she "promised" to hide her feelings. She recapitulated the event and successfully accomplished the magical process of self-healing. For the first time since she was five years old, she feels relief and freedom. Now she is able to stop the painful routine of repressing the expression of her feelings. After doing this for the first time, her relationships begin to improve. She blossoms.

But there is a catch in all of this: If she does not start practicing not-doings right after having recapitulated the events of her life, chances are that after a period of time she could lose what she has earned.

While doings may be understood to be like those actions that are congruent with our personal history and reinforce the ego and this personal history, not-doings, in general, may be understood to be like those actions that are not congruent with our personal history. Therefore, the continuous and careful practice of not-doings tends to produce a destructuring of the ego—which leads to discovering what we are beyond the fantasy of the ego. Not-doings, when done in a balanced way, produce freedom.

In the context of recapitulation, the not-doings are those actions congruent with the process of healing, similar to the way the doings are congruent with the process of energetic illness. In Mary's case the doing was never to express what she felt. The not-doing would be to purposefully express her feelings every time she has the chance. She would practice this not just because she needs to but as a part of her strategy to make permanent the provisional healing of the recapitulation work. These kinds of actions are also known as purposeful or liberated acts and are the requisite to achieving definitive restoration (see figure 7).

Fig. 7.
Definitive restoration after a period of liberated acts

Obviously, the practice of not-doings must be balanced with a necessary dose of common sense. This means not taking the practice of not-doings to such an extent as to engage in problems bigger than the ones we are solving.

Finally, to conclude this chapter, figure 8 illustrates the whole process of energetic illness due to emotional interactions and the process of healing through recapitulation. Notice how the recapitulation process is the reverse of the process of energetic damage.

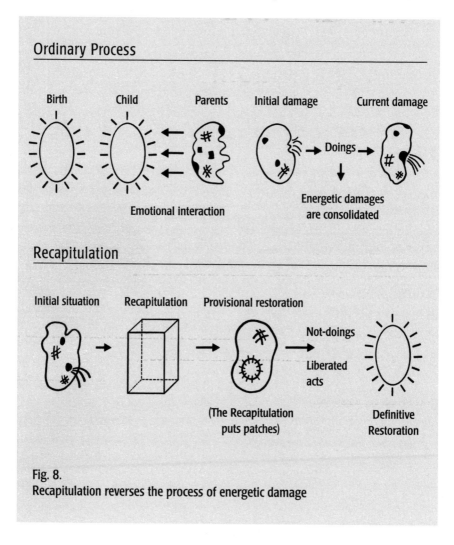

Fig. 8.
Recapitulation reverses the process of energetic damage

5

Who Should Do Recapitulation?

Suggestions and Precautions for Special Cases

One important question that is asked in some of my presentations on recapitulation is whether or not potential risk is involved in the recapitulation process. This is an important question, and the general answer is no—this is a very safe practice and there is no potential risk in carrying it out. Nevertheless, there are special cases that require comment.

Let us approach this theme with the most frequently asked questions, followed by answers.

Q. Are there any risks in practicing recapitulation?

A. There is no physical or mental risk in the practice of recapitulation beyond the normal risks associated with common activities such as walking, taking a shower, and dancing. Of course, you may have an accident while engaging in any of those common activities, but the accident would not be related to a potential risk belonging to that specific activity. With recapitulation it is just the same; in terms of risk it is a normal activity without any potential risk related to the activity itself. Just as with dancing, meditation, or jogging, you should have some level of good health to be able to do it.

Q. What about the states of nonordinary reality, like those of deep recapitulation?

A. It is true that you are going to switch to a different state of awareness, but there is no risk involved in doing so for the simple reason that those possibilities are part of our normal capacities just as seeing, hearing, and thinking are normal for us. The fact that we usually do not know how to use or enter into those other states of awareness does not mean that there is anything wrong or risky in doing so.

While you are recapitulating, the entire scene of what is surrounding you may change. You may hear voices, see visions, have physical sensations. You may see the devil itself, so to speak, and there is no danger in that. Recapitulation is a trip—a trip toward your self, a trip to the hidden side of your self. But it is a safe round-trip ticket. No matter what you see, it is part of the experience, and you are going to get back to your ordinary awareness. The important part is how much self-healing you can do while in the other side.

Q. Is there any danger in spending a period of time that could be hours inside a wooden box?

A. No, there is not, because you make your box with adequate air intakes. What you are looking for by entering a box is isolation from the world so you may focus your whole attention on the act of recapitulation. There are other advantages as well that will be discussed when we get to the technical procedures for recapitulation.

Q. Who should practice recapitulation? Is recapitulation recommended for all people with no exceptions?

A. In general terms, recapitulation as a natural process is going to be part of every single human being's existence. Actually, we have talked already about the recapitulation of a dying person and about spontaneous recapitulation. The specific practice of the techniques to recapitulate deliberately are recommended for almost everyone having a past and having an energetic body that has not always been treated in the most energetically healthy way. This means almost every adult in modern society. The only prerequisite is that you have no special physical or mental condition that could be inconvenient, in terms of what recapitulation techniques involve. These would be exceptional cases, which I will describe below.

Basically, recapitulation *is not* recommended if you are too sick or too healthy. Recapitulation *is* recommended for those of us included in what I call the pathology of normal people: those who are not suffering extreme problems in everyday life but who at the same time are dealing with a continual wasting of energy because of bad habits acquired in the past. Those who are far above or far under that normality would not urgently need recapitulation; some of them could create more trouble by doing it. Let's discuss some specific cases. I'll begin with the ones on the happy side.

Children

Children in general have a good energetic condition, so in terms of energy the practice of recapitulation would be futile. Besides, the recapitulation techniques involve steps and procedures that require control and discipline not in accordance with children's developmental capabilities.

In the case of children with special problems, including those related to traumatic experiences of their past, it should be clear that we have not researched the use of recapitulation in this group; therefore, my view is that there is not enough evidence yet to recommend practicing these techniques in a safe way with children. Future research may provide new procedures in this field.

Teenagers

I have had a few cases of adolescents practicing recapitulation with some success. Most of the time, however, it is not that effective for the following reasons:

Some of these young people are in very good energetic shape because they have not suffered from significant emotional traumas, so there is not much they need to recapitulate. They have had a good life from the energy perspective. Remember that old saying: If it's not broken, don't fix it!

The other extreme is also possible. One of the existential diseases of modern Western technological societies is what I call the decrepit youth syndrome. I have seen many young people, under or around the age of twenty, whose energetic condition is similar to that of a very old, sick person. Their bodies are so tired and weak, and the worst part is that their souls are old, sick, and tired as well. In most cases, these young people have been passing through extremely difficult situations related to family disintegration, solitude, drugs, violence, and so forth.

My experience with these kinds of cases has been that some of them helped themselves through the practice of recapitulation, while others were still not ready. Maybe there was too much anger inside preventing them from seeing where the enemy was. Maybe they still wanted to explore everything, so they did not feel like focusing and committing themselves to a single practice (Recapitulation is not the kind of healing practice that I have found appropriate for these kinds of people) I have found it more useful to invite them to participate in some of our other workshops, where physical activities and "adventures" are included, such as our workshops in the woods, jungle, and desert.

Healthy "Tonals"

I use this expression to talk about those kinds of special people who have found their own way to live using their energy in a very healthy way. I am talking about those few who do not fight with life but dance with it. Let us say that they do not have significant energetic injuries in their energetic body or if they had them, they have already healed them.

For these happy, creative, and productive people, recapitulation is not an urgent matter but instead a pending issue. Nevertheless, there is no way to know what is going to arise during recapitulation. Hence, a word of caution: Sometimes the attitude that "I am great, and I have a great life" is the mask of a gigantic lie. In these cases recapitulation is a matter of life-or-death importance.

But let us suppose that we are talking about those who have no big problems coming from their past. Maybe they are having a happy, healthy, and intense life—but they are not perfect. It is not possible to have everything under control all the time. Sometimes things go wrong, and we need to recapitulate specific events. For them, the last techniques of this book related to recapitulating single events could be useful.

Now let us see when recapitulation is not recommended due to special problems.

Those with Mental Disorders

One of the things that recapitulation does is to alter the perception of the practitioner. Actually, one of the major problems of people nowadays is living under the fixation of just one way of perceiving, which is controlled by the ego. Therefore, part of the methodology in all my work in general has to do with ways of taking people away from normal perception. The idea is to take them to the other side, so they can get the perspective to balance the incomplete vision they usually have.

Now what happens to those people with mental disorders whose perception is already altered? What if we take them into practices that intend to alter the perception? The result is that they can become even more confused and lost.

This is why I say that recapitulation is not recommended for people with mental disorders. What they need is not an altered state of awareness but to find their way back to "normal" perception." There is no reason to move the carpet under their feet, because the carpet under their feet is already moving too much. They need different practices that help them engage in everyday reality.

One problem of many confused people with mental disorders is the influence of shamanic or esoteric issues, which they connect with in order to convince themselves that what they see is the product of some kind of gift that makes them special human beings) Some of these people really require professional help, but they do not know it.

The worst part is that some groups do not care, as long as they have clients. The weirder the person is, the more often some of these groups say: *Cool! You are so special!* That is why you should never abdicate the use of your own criteria and common sense; they enable you to avoid becoming another victim of those kinds of cult groups.

It is clear that recapitulation is not recommended for people with schizophrenia, psychotic deliriums, suicidal depression, and the like—the clinical cases of mental illness. But where is the thin line that separates the clinical cases from those that are not?

Many people ask questions such as: "I have been receiving medical treatment for depression, but now I am okay. Can I do recapitulation?" or, "I am under psychiatric treatment and taking pills. Is recapitulation recommended for me?" There is no way to provide a general answer for these and similar questions because each case is different, but there are some helpful guidelines.

If you are passing through an intense depression or having recurrent suicidal thoughts, recapitulation is not recommended for you. This is different from the people who say, "I am depressed," meaning they are worried or upset in relation to temporary problems in their life. For those people recapitulation is okay. What we are dealing with is the distinction between the word *depressed* in the vernacular sense, meaning basically "to be worried," and the medical concept of depression, which implies a series of symptoms, is chronic, and includes organic disorders.

So my general answer to the questions mentioned above is: Ask your doctor. Explain to him or her exactly what you would be doing during recapitulation, and the doctor will give you a more precise answer as to whether or not this kind of practice is safe and suitable for you.

Drug Users

For reasons similar to the ones that apply to people with mental disorders, recapitulation is not recommended for people involved with drugs. I am not talking about those who have used drugs at some time in their life, but rather about regular drug consumers. Drugs alter perception in an un-controlled way; an individual using them with some regularity has his or her perception altered, whether or not that person is aware of it. The harder the drugs, the higher the risk involved in practices for the left side.

People using drugs are straddling a delicate line, which I call the point of no return. Our mental health is a fragile system that is not invulner-able. I must say it loud and clear: I have seen many young people with their fuses blown because they didn't know when it was time to stop. Some of them had good spiritual aims, but they were not aware of the risk they were taking. This is one of the reasons for always discouraging people from using drugs as a way to look for *the other side*. Recapitulation is a very safe technique for this search, but not when combined with the use of drugs.

In this discussion of the use of drugs in relation to recapitulation, I should add a comment about the use of "soft" drugs, such as marijuana and tobacco.

Marijuana

I am sorry to disappoint some of you, but I have found in my research in this field that marijuana consumers doing recapitulation lose about 50 percent of the results—a big disadvantage in a challenge that is not easy to begin with.

Some people use marijuana under the presumption that this drug will help them to connect with the other side. On the contrary, even with the apparent extra sensibility that marijuana use produces, the fact is that the drug stimulates the center of reason, which means that it is a right-side drug. Because of this, one of its typical effects is to stimulate thinking; you can be thinking and thinking the very same thing again and again without being aware of this. Or you may have common, silly thoughts, even though you feel that your thoughts are the most extraordinary discoveries. The simple truth comes after the effects have gone: You and your life are not better at all. Your supposedly brilliant realizations have gone, just as the smoke has.

To say it in one word, the use of marijuana is an *obstacle* to achieving the left-side awareness that is an important part of recapitulation.

Tobacco

Even though tobacco does not stimulate the mind as marijuana does, its effects on the breathing process make its use almost catastrophic for recapitulation. Those who use tobacco during the recapitulation period lose between 20 and 50 percent of their results.

Breathing is one of the magical tools used for restoring our energetic body. If our breathing system is blocked because of nicotine, there is not much we can do to succeed in the recapitulation process.

If you are interested in recapitulation, but you are an occasional or frequent consumer of marijuana or tobacco, you should stop using them. You need from fifteen to sixty days to cleanse your body of the effects of those drugs before you start your recapitulation. It is hoped that with the extra energy gained through recapitulation, you will not go back to smoking again.

Sonia's Story

I want to finish this part by telling the story of a young woman who in one of our recapitulation workshops did not respect our restrictions for drug consumers and people with mental disorders. It was the only time in my experience that a person with either condition lied to sneak into a recapitulation workshop.

We were working in an old monastery in Europe. This monastery is now a private property in the countryside, quiet and isolated, very appropriate for a group working on recapitulation.

The woman who my story is about was close to thirty years old. For this workshop, as for all our workshops, we asked those in the group to fill out a questionnaire regarding medical problems or restrictions to avoid any risk for the participants. Some of the questions were very specific regarding mental disorders and the use of drugs. Sonia* responded to the questions in the same way as those in the rest of the group; she said she did not use drugs and did not have any kind of mental disorder. She lied in both answers.

We had been working for a few days, and the process was becoming intense for everybody. Suddenly, Sonia began speaking incoherently and making exaggerated gestures. Both her strange way of talking and the amazing expressions on her face began to scare everybody. The more she was able to confuse and scare people, the more she seemed happy to do it. In the beginning most people thought that maybe her strange behavior had to do with her process of recapitulation. Then, as her behavior become more strange and uncontrolled, everybody grew worried.

At first I tried to talk to her, asking her what she was experiencing. Her answers were complete nonsense. I told her that if she was not able to control herself, then she would be required to stop working with the group. She responded by challenging me and started doing everything except what was required of her. When I saw her at night, wandering around outside the venue, frightening everybody, I knew she was in real danger.

I decided to call her family to explain the problem we were having with her. They did not seem too surprised. Her mother said, "Yes, I told her she

---

*The name has been changed to protect the identity of the actual person.

should not be doing that work. She's had schizophrenic episodes—her father suffered from schizophrenia—and she has problems with drugs."

Her boyfriend told me that two days before, when the recapitulation workshop had already begun, she went to his house and took a combination of heroin and cocaine. He had tried everything to make her stop using drugs but with no success.

I asked him to come and pick her up, but he said, "I can't do that. She is stronger than I am, and I can't control her."

Oh, Lord! I thought, *we have problems!*

"Has she been under medical treatment?" I asked.

"Yes, I can give you her doctor's telephone number."

So I called the doctor and he said, "Listen. According to what you are describing, she is experiencing a schizophrenic episode, probably caused by the drugs, not sleeping well, and the physical exercises you're describing. She's had these kinds of problems in the past. She's in real danger and may harm herself. What you should do is take her to the nearest hospital as soon as possible. She's not able to understand what's going on with her right now, so she's not going to accept leaving. You should take her to the hospital by force." He repeated, "She's in real danger."

I certainly did not like what I heard, but there was no way to escape. I accepted my destiny and committed myself to doing my best to protect her and to protect the group.

My old friend and collaborator, Manolo, was there with me. We divided the work. I was going to continue working with the group while he would do the hard part: take Sonia to the hospital, using force if necessary.

I took the group to the house of a group member while Manolo remained at the monastery trying to convince Sonia to rest, to see her family, or to see her doctor. Nothing seemed to work. When she heard the word *doctor* she became furious and cursed Manolo. So he started with Plan B, to stalk her and trick her in some way, in order to take her to the hospital. He was trying not to have to use Plan C, physical battle with the strong Sonia. Manolo's additional concern had to do with a revelation from Sonia's mother when we were talking about her daughter: Sonia's boyfriend had AIDS.

What if she bites me? Manolo thought.

Anyway, being the impeccable warrior that he is, Manolo accepted the challenge he was facing. Since she had rejected all his invitations to go into the nearby city for breakfast, Manolo said, "I'm so hungry, but I don't know what to do. Victor told me to stay with you at all times, so I can't go for breakfast." That seemed to touch Sonia, because she said, "I can accompany you while you have your breakfast." So they left.

After they got out of the car, Manolo pretended to be looking for a specific restaurant where they made "exquisite fried eggs" and rejected all the other restaurants they passed. He was actually walking closer and closer to the hospital while distracting Sonia with the story about the restaurant. When they finally came close to the main door of the hospital, Sonia discovered the trap. She tried to run, but in that moment Manolo was right behind her, ready to act, and he firmly embraced her. She resisted and tried to fight for a few seconds, then relaxed her body in the next moment. He carried her for a few yards, to where hospital personnel were ready to receive her, having gotten a call from her doctor explaining the situation.

Inside the hospital a friendly female doctor met Sonia and took her into an examining room. Sonia gave Manolo a last look of hatred and disappeared behind the door. For some time Sonia hated us. Months later, however, she sent a letter to our offices in Mexico, expressing thanks for the loving way we had protected her when she was in trouble.

This was the only time in twenty years of workshops and twelve years of recapitulation workshops that we have had a situation like this. I include Sonia's story here to make very clear the importance of not entering into practices for the left side when mental disorders or the use of drugs is involved.

PART 2

The Techniques: How to Do the Recapitulation

6

AVP Ten-Steps Technique for Recapitulation

B ecause it is a natural act, recapitulation can be achieved through a variety of means. In the first part of this book I have talked about spontaneous recapitulation, which can be achieved accidentally in many different circumstances.

Corporeal, or body, connections with the past are an important element of several psychotherapy systems. Likewise, corporeal manipulation and deep massage can bring to the surface emotions and feelings from our hidden past. Catharsis techniques using painful physical postures or techniques of dancing or jumping in a rhythmic and continual way may also lead to reliving emotions that have been repressed for a long time. Some of them could be connected with events from our remote past. Breathing techniques (such as allotropic breathing, rebirthing, and primal therapy) also open doors for the flowing of repressed feelings.

All these techniques, when administered with expertise, could be very helpful for people getting closer to themselves. Nevertheless, none of these techniques systematically addresses the spectrum of relevant events of our past in a very precise way and through an integral process to heal the energetic body. Some of them are very good at bringing out feelings; others, in calling forth memories. Some are useful for temporary relief of an emotional pain carried for a long time. Most of them are too focused on the intense explosive expression of emotions, without having a detailed and complete plan to handle on purpose the subsequent stages of a process of healing. When this happens the individual, who is very impressed by the intensity of the emotional expression, has the expectation that this is enough for overcoming the problem. Later on, that person discovers it was not enough; something was missing.

It is my view that recapitulation is the most complete technique ever developed to heal our lives systematically from the damage we are carrying from the past.

My first design of the technique, Recapitulation in a Box, as presented in my book *The Teachings of Don Carlos,** was a free interpretation and re-creation based on the technique of recapitulation presented in the sixth book of Castaneda, *The Eagle's Gift.* The technique presented in that book was the outline by which I was inspired to create the first version of the recapitulation technique, which was used in our research in that field.

This first version of the technique was based on three main elements: a list of events to recapitulate, a wooden box in which to recapitulate, and a set of two different kinds of breathing related to recovering or releasing energy. The outline of the procedure was to recount in writing all the events of your past with the result being the creation of a list of events that would be useful to achieve two main goals:

1. To force the body to remember
2. To serve as the "travel guide" for the subsequent recapitulation exercises

---

*Victor Sanchez, *The Teachings of Don Carlos.*

Once the list was done, the next step was to build a box of wood with a door for entering. Inside the box the practitioner would begin remembering the events included on the list, focusing on the feelings that were present during each event. Finally, to "fix" the energetic damage generated from that event, the practitioner would use special techniques of breathing designed for that purpose.

Through the years, we have developed all the detailed steps and requirements to do the recapitulation—for instance, the duration of recapitulation sessions, the most appropriate place and time to do them, how to organize the events, what to do inside the box, and exercises to be done before and in between recapitulation to push the body to remember. Actually, what started as a basic, simple process has developed into a very complex, articulated, and sophisticated program of work. In the beginning we saw recapitulation as a series of procedures focusing on the left side of awareness. Now we are dealing with a process that integrates the two sides of our consciousness.

All the steps of the old technique have been completed and refined with the inclusion of parts that were missing in the beginning. Aside from the three main elements mentioned above, some others of great importance have been incorporated:

- Procedures and suggestions to elaborate on the list
- Specific steps to be carried out inside the box
- Techniques to solve obstacles on the go
- What to do after the work within the box
- How to apply and reinforce the results of the experiences within the box in everyday life

As has been shown, the work after the box is one of the most important elements of the whole recapitulation, to support and consolidate what has been achieved with the list and within the box.

In this new vision the elements of recapitulation could be divided into two series, as follows.

Elements of Recapitulation

Left Side–Nagual–Energetic Body

The recapitulation box

Body memories

Breathing techniques

Energetic command

Rituals

Energetic body restoration

Right Side–Tonal–Normal Awareness

List of events

Ordinary memories

Choosing purposeful acts

Decision making

Talking about the process (feedback)

Carrying out purposeful acts

In this list we may notice that the work of recapitulation includes areas to be done from the right-side awareness and others to be done from or in left-side awareness. This means that instead of trying to complete a process based only in the rational mind or focused just in the "magical" procedures, we are going to cover both sides, which is in keeping with our nature as dual beings.

In relation to the recapitulation techniques, it has been said that rituals are not necessary or even convenient for modern people. It has been said that rituals belong to ancient times, and are not required nowadays.

It has been said that rituals simply darken the process. A comment here to refute these ideas is appropriate.

Rituals are, in fact, related to the left side, the side of *silent knowledge*. Their purpose is to focus our attention so we can connect with the *otherness*. Looking for the contact and reconnection with our other side is an essential part of our process of reintegration. Therefore, the practice of rituals is a useful means that helps in achieving that purpose.

It is absurd to relate these rituals to dark visions or fantasies about "black sorcery." A balanced and powerful ritual requires deep concentration and a sense of openness either to what is out there—the universe of fields of energy (e.g., the big *poderios* of the world)—or to what is inside us—the inner space (e.g., the hidden memories of the energetic body). And sometimes it requires an openness to both. What makes rituals so useful in some moments of the work is their capacity to help us cross from the rational mind to the more open space of silent knowledge.

Sometimes imitating rituals that belong to practices of indigenous peoples is not a good idea because many of the elements of the rituals are connected with *their* cultural background and *their* way of life. For instance, the Wirrarika, the indigenous people with whom I am connected, are peasants. The farming cycle is present in some of their rituals. We in the cities may also be peasants, but we work in offices, factories, institutions, schools, and so on. Consequently, our rituals should be connected with our own world. That is why we have been working to create a translation for some of the rituals and procedures we have learned among the Wirrarika. And it works!

Finally, like procedures to focus our attention, rituals don't need to be bizarre. Simplicity, sobriety, and heart are the best qualities of a ritual among the new Toltecs.

The whole process is ordered as follows:

1. What you do before working in the box (i.e., the list and building the list)

2. What you do inside the box (i.e., procedures to work on each event on the list)
3. What you do after working in the box (i.e., incorporating the results into your everyday life and reinforcing the healing)

In the following chapters each of the related steps will be explained in detail. For better understanding of each step, however, it is important now that you have a general idea or outline of the process. To help you with this, here is the list of steps that constitute the AVP Ten-Steps Technique for Recapitulation.

AVP Ten-Steps Technique for Recapitulation

Stage	Step	Action
Before the box	1.	List for recapitulation
	2.	Building the box

Stage	Step	Action
Inside the box	3.	Starting breathing
	4.	Seeing the event
	5.	Reliving the event
	6.	Energetic restoration
	7.	Decision making
	8.	Dreaming not-doings

Stage	Step	Action
After the box	9.	Accomplishing not-doings
	10.	Continuity

Usually, you will create the list and the box at the same time. You will use the procedures inside the box for every event or series of events you recapitulate. Steps 9 and 10 (the not-doings and continuity) that you engage in after your work in the box should be present and remain as part of your normal life.

It is important for you to remember that the meaning we give here to the term *not-doing* is very specific in relation to recapitulation. While *not-doing* is a very open term that could be related to the not-doings of the perception or the not-doings of the personal self,* the not-doing included in the list of steps here means "liberated acts," which are the not-doings related to recapitulation. This clarification is important to avoid confusion for those who were already familiar with the term *not-doing*.

With the list you help yourself to remember and begin to "pinch" the memory of the other side. Then you build your box, to have an ideal place in which to recapitulate the events of your life. Inside the box you pick one event from your list; then you relive it to do the corresponding healing through the steps that follow. You are going to do the same with the rest of the events on your list in as many recapitulation sessions as you need. As a way to complete your work, you are going to carry out *liberated actions* after your work in the box.

For example, let's say you were recapitulating events that led you to plant the rancor toward your father that has been with you for many years. Let us say that the rancor has been blocking your need to express your love for him, which is also real within you. Then you recapitulate the events during which you made that promise (i.e., to hate your father). You relive those events, you heal them, and you feel better. After this, to prevent the energetic "patch," or the recapitulation, from failing, you practice deliberate actions (not-doings) that correspond to the work you did inside the box. These liberated actions are so named because before the

*For more detailed information on this matter, see *The Teachings of Don Carlos*, by Victor Sanchez.

recapitulation you were not able to do such things, but after the process you are free to do them. Examples of this would be embracing your father without expectation of reward, talking to him more often, inviting him for a friendly dinner, telling him that you love him.

I know you may have many questions about aspects of the process that are not clear to you, but they will be answered when we fully review each step. In addition, there are more steps and sub-steps, such as the ritual of burning your box after finishing the work, which will be presented ahead.

Finally, a short comment about the name of the technique we are going to learn about: I chose to name the technique the AVP Ten-Steps Technique for Recapitulation, instead of (for instance) Victor Sanchez's Technique, because it is not only my personal work that is behind it. It is the work of many people who have been part of AVP workshops. It is the work of the team of instructors of AVP. It is a collective creation coming from a collective experience.

The bottom line is that AVP is not just another company, and it is much more than just an organization. AVP is a collective dream that has been taking many people, including us, inside the dream. AVP is the dream of the new Toltecs. It is the dream of going back to what we are, a dream about going back to join and work together with the flow of life that is moving the entire universe—a dream of mystery, fellowship, and freedom.

And yes, there is room in this dream for many more.

Welcome.

7

Step 1: The List

The list of recapitulation comprises the events you are going to recapitulate inside the box, which are basically the meaningful events of your entire life.

There are three main purposes for creating this list:

1. to trigger the internal process of recapitulation, by forcing ourselves to focus on the task of remembering and reliving
2. to help the practitioner to recover hidden memories
3. to function as a practical tool so we may know what events we are going to recapitulate and in what order we are going to do it

I have written about the list for recapitulation in *The Teachings of Don Carlos*. Those who have read that book will find this new proposal of how to work with the list much simpler but at the same time much deeper. Instead of a complex system with four columns and many areas, or categories, of recapitulation, what we have now is essentially a first column with the names of the meaningful people of our life and a second column with all the significant events we have lived with them.

Theoretically the list of events to recapitulate should include all the events we have been involved in during our entire life. But if we were to consider just ten events per day in the life of a thirty-five-year-old person, we would end up with a list of 127,750 items. Besides the time required simply to name that many events, try to imagine the work involved in being able to remember all of them. From this point of view, the list of events would result in a virtually impossible task.

The simple truth is that in our list of events we do not need to include all the events of our life, just those that are significant in terms of energy in one way or another. The meaning of the word *significant* in relation to our list of events is very open. First of all, significant in terms of energy does not mean what seems significant for our personal ego. On the contrary, *significant* in this context means that our energetic body was affected in such a way that the effects of that event are still present in our current energetic condition and, therefore, in the life we are living at the present.

There are some special events whose significance is obvious to us already. I am talking about the events we can remember as the ones that determined our life to be the way it has been. Those events certainly should be included on our list, but they do not cover even a small part of what was significant in our life in terms of the energy we left or the intruder energy that was left in our field of energy.

This means that by making a very detailed list we are going to include almost everything, so that through the entire work we can chase the meaningful events that are ultimately relevant for the purpose of this work.

So that you can have a simple idea of what kind of events are the ones we need to recapitulate the most, the following list gives examples:

- Events during which you made promises that changed your life
- Events during which your vision about sex and affection was created or modified
- Events during which you resigned or lost in any manner something that was an authentic expression of your self
- Events during which your personal repetitive fears were implanted

- Events with painful emotional interactions
- Events of great joy, which are your hidden memory about happiness and how to achieve it
- Events involving your sexual experiences
- Events involving the meaningful relationships of your life
- Events about which you feel shame simply in remembering them
- Events related to the things you have been hiding from others' eyes
- Events in which you can find parts of yourself that you normally think are completely lost
- Events involving pain for the loss of somebody you loved
- Events involving joy from loving others
- Events during which the Great Spirit made a gesture to you
- Events during which you let your spirit express itself with no restraints
- Events during which you betrayed your self or others

This list of examples could continue endlessly; these are just a handful, but they may give you an idea of what could be a significant event in terms of energy.

Now we still have two problems to solve. Number one, how are you going to recognize those events you do not know are significant? Number two, the number of events still seems to be too large. Where are you going to find the time to recall and then recapitulate so many events?

To solve the first problem, what we do is try to include all the events that come to our mind and seem to be significant in any way, aside from the important ones. Now what do I mean when I say "significant, aside from the important ones"? Basically, important events are the ones we already consider important, like the ones presented in the list of examples above. Significant events are those that are not quite as important but could have some significance.

For instance, let us imagine this: When I was seven years old, my aunt took me with her to buy groceries. On our way to the store we came upon a fair, where we stopped for a while. It was a very nice day and the first time I had gone somewhere with my aunt. Now just based on the facts, this was not an important event in my life. Nevertheless, I am going to include it on my list as a significant event because it comes to my mind as something I remember about my aunt. On the other hand, I would not list as separate events my ride on the merry-go-round and when we bought popcorn. Nor would I include on my list when we came back home and I ate my dinner of cookies and milk. I would not put these small events on my list unless something really special for me happened during them.

Certainly, there is not anything like a precise line separating the important events from the small, insignificant ones. It is an arbitrary selection we make based on our own feeling and discernment. Even if it seems confusing, the fact is that once we have started the work, we will find the sense of how to do it. There is no way to say a final word in terms of this event being right or that event being wrong. We are talking about a process, and once we engage in it, things will tend to flow naturally.

Now to solve the second problem: How do we deal with the enormous number of significant events? How much are we going to write?

What we are looking for is to recapitulate not all the events, but only the ones that we need to recapitulate. Since we may not identify these merely by thinking which events might be the ones we need to heal, we must cover the whole spectrum of our entire life. But this is still too much, so we need to organize our list in relation to some areas (categories). For instance, we may start by making a list of all the people we have known and then write down all the meaningful events we lived with each of them.

This is still a very big list. Trying to dig into our past to remember all those people is still work that would take a great deal of time. Chances are that we would get desperate and then exhausted trying to remember all that before we could get through even half the list. To avoid this, we subdivided the area of people we have known into subareas or preliminary lists that will be easier to track later and integrate into one complete list.

The following is a suggested list. You can use all of the areas, exclude some, or add others, according to the kind of life you have had.

Formulating Your List

a. Make a List of Areas or Sub-lists That Will Be Useful for You

Your list of lists could include any number from ten to approximately twenty areas. At the same time, while some areas are common for almost everybody (such as family), others are going to be related specifically to you. The italicized areas are a must, because as a general rule they have strong energetic consequences for everybody. Note that the area *Partners* and *People I have had sex with* may overlap, but there are times when we may have sexual encounters with people who are not partners or we might be with a partner with whom we never have sex, so it is important to include both areas, even if some names could be listed in both.

1. *Relatives*

2. *Friends*

3. *Partners*

4. *People I have had sex with*

5. Companions in schools

6. Work mates

7. People related to my spiritual quest

8. People related to the world of music (if you are a musician— you may adjust this category to your personal area of interest)

Sex and Energy

Because I know this is a theme with implications that are very confusing and controversial, I would like to comment on why a recapitulation of our sexual encounters is important.

- Sex is important in terms of energy because it involves the exchange of a large amount of energy.

- It is important because our sexual impulse is one of our most basic instincts, which means that it is present during our entire life, whether or not we are aware of it.

- The relationship between sex and affection can be so strong and confusing that the conflict among what we want, what we think we want, and what we have been told we should want creates conditions guaranteed to waste a lot of energy during our sexual experiences.

- I disagree with the vision that presents sex as something that is always wrong. Sex is one of the most beautiful experiences we may have, as long as we remain close to our own heart and we listen to our heart's voice, rather than to the voice of the moralist who always finds a way to create fear in order to control others.

- Pretending that by not having sex at all our energetic body will be healthier is like trying to save or increase our energy through not dancing, singing, practicing a sport, or climbing a mountain, based on the argument that those activities consume a great deal of energy. What damages us is the empty sex, when you are not entirely present and willing to jump into the mystery of leaving behind your ego, to disappear into the experience of *us*.

- Empty sex is happening too often in most people's lives— and it is certainly weakening them. However, sex, passion, and deep love combined will open doors to the magical side of our being. The challenge is this: Without being close to our own heart, how can we become close to others?

- Western society's approach to sex is sick. On the one hand television and other media are constantly drawing our attention to sex to entice us to buy something. On the other hand there is an almost ever-present sense of guilt and sin associated with sex. Our ideas of love are contaminated by show business. We have been listening to the stories of television and movies and to society's hypocritical moral values regarding sex and love for so long that without being aware of it we have accepted that sickness.

- The only way to find our path to a healthier experience of love and sex is to stop listening to those sick advisers, those propagators of fear, and start listening attentively to our own heart. In the depth of our silent knowledge, each of us knows exactly what we need. Our task is to find our own way to return there. A thorough recapitulation of our sexual life is a good starting point.

As you can see, the common theme of the areas on your list is *people*, because our energetic story is a story related to people. In one way or another we relate to people all the time—and that is the story of our lives.

Nevertheless, there are meaningful events that may not be connected to the presence of someone else—events that you originate or that happen to you when you are alone. Maybe you have already guessed that there is no way to be alone, because there are always other fields of energy surrounding us. This is not significant from the point of view of the average person, but it is quite important from the Toltec point of view, in which all our connections are significant, not only the ones involving other people.

For instance, if you have a close relationship with nature, you may have had very important events of interaction with a mountain, a river, or the ocean. Even if you have never considered nature to be important in your life, you have been interacting with the fields of energy of the natural world all the time. This is similar to what happens to those who say that they do not have any relationship with their parents, for whatever reasons. The simple truth is that whether or not they are aware of this, an apparent lack of interaction is itself a kind of interaction. If you think you have no relationship with nature, your ignorance of your connection with nature is the kind of relationship you have with it.

So it is convenient that you include two more areas or sub-lists that might be called:

9. Events that happen while being alone
10. Events of interactions with nonhuman fields of energy

Please understand that when I indicate an area regarding interactions with nonhuman fields of energy. I am not suggesting you should recapitulate strange dreams or any kind of experiences when you perhaps saw something that you thought might be a phantom, spirit, alien, or other strange phenomenon. Rather, I am talking about much clearer experiences involving interaction with the natural world—for example, particular times when you engaged in an activity that takes place in nature, or specific instances when you experienced a spiritual or deep human–nature connection such as those that people sometimes have while mountaineering or trekking.*

b. Write the Names of the People Related to Each List Area

Writing the names of the people in each specific list area will make it easier for you to remember them. Parts of this task will be completed in a few minutes (for instance, writing names of relatives in a small family), while others may take days (writing the names of your sex partners, perhaps), depending on the features of your own life.

In this part of the process you are not going to write down what you have lived with all those people; it's merely a list of names. As a general rule, for this and the upcoming lists, you are going to follow the simple method of writing what comes to your mind in the first try. Do not force

---

*Certainly, this comment could lead to this question: How do we tell the difference between a clear experience of interaction with nonhuman fields of energy and an experience that is useless? I have to deal with this question often in my workshops, because during the night we do a number of activities outdoors that deal with mystery. At these times someone always comes to me to ask something similar to the following:

"I guess I saw a strange shadow in the bushes; it was like a human shape, with dark spots on his face, and it was sort of blinking, as if it was making a gesture to me. What was that?"

I have no idea; you were the one who saw it. You tell me.

"I don't know. I just want to know what its meaning is. . . ."

I don't know. I suppose the meaning is that you think you saw a shadow among the bushes in the shape of a man with dark spots on his face, and he blinked at you.

"But what should I do?"

I don't know. What do you want to do?

"Nothing. I just wondered whether or not that shadow was a special sign or omen for me."

Well, it had no meaning that you can clearly feel in your heart; if it had, you would not need to ask me about it—so I would say that it is not an omen for you. Or maybe it's a useless omen, in which case the best thing we can do is forget it so that our attention is not distracted from the moment when a real omen might arrive.

I know this kind of answer can be disappointing. Why? Because some people are desperate to see the strange things they have read about in books; they have a secret fantasy that seeing such strange things indicates that they are "special." What we have in these situations are cases of the popular game of self-importance, of trying to be "somebody," which is one of the basic compulsions of the ego.

yourself to try to recall every person from every season of your life; just work steadily up to the present. To avoid getting stuck in any period, remember that you can go back to the beginning of your list for a more meticulous search up to the present. Repeat this system of successive searches several times. Every time you do another review of your list, more names are going to come to your memory. The main point here is not to stop your work because you are not able to remember part of what should be on your list. Keep going and leave that blank space for later.

c. Organize All the Names into One Big List

Now merge all the lists you have into one. Here you can choose between two different strategies: the *by age stages* method and the *by area method*. Both are useful and should be selected according to the way you have organized your program for recapitulation.

The first method is recommended for intensive periods of recapitulation, which means that you are going to recapitulate daily, several hours each day, for several weeks. The second is recommended for a program involving recapitulation sessions that will be spread over a longer period of time—for example, you will be recapitulating on the weekends or in three- to four-hour sessions, two or three times a week. In chapter 12 we will examine this option in detail.

In the *by age stages* method, you will combine all the names from all your lists into one big list. Next, you will arrange each person on this master list according to the season of your life when your relationship took place. Names coming from different lists will merge in the same section of the list, if they were present at the same stage of your life. You can organize the names by the age you were when you met each person and had a relationship with him or her. For instance, all the relationships of your adulthood are going to be together in the same section of your list, as will be those of your youth, adolescence, childhood, and infancy. You may work by arranging the names from the present to the past or from the past to the present, whichever is easier for you in order to remember.

The *by area* method consists of organizing the names chronologically but keeping them in their original lists. Then, in order to make one big list, you simply choose the order of your sub-lists. Which area do you want to work with and finish before you work with the next one? Here, the criteria you use will vary depending on your own needs and circumstances: Which area is more urgent for you to work with? How much time do you have to invest in your list? Maybe you need to choose the main areas first. In which areas are the events related to that part of yourself that you need to rescue?

The point here is to choose an order that will make your list work. For example, you may decide to work first with your sentimental relationships (partners), then with your parents, then with your sexual partners, and so on. That resulting order, whatever it is, comprises your one big list.

d. Write Down the Events

Now you will write the names of the most significant events that you lived with each person. Start with the first person on your list, writing down all the meaningful events in relation to him or her. You may start from the moment when you first met that person to the last moment of the relationship or vice versa, whichever is easier for you.

It is important to know that you should not describe what happened during each event; you are simply going to include a few words that remind you of the event. For instance, if you are writing about the events that involve your sister and you remember a fight with her, do not describe what happened then; merely write "fight in school with Linda." Also, it is important that you do not engage in analyzing the event—simply register it, because the list is an exercise not in analytic thinking, but of observation. Observe and register—it's as simple as that.

After you have listed all the meaningful events related to the first person, do the same for the following person, and so on, until you have finished all the people on your list. Once again, you may start recapitulation as soon as you have finished listing the events from one or more areas, instead of waiting to finish all your areas. While this is not the best option, it is possible. On the one hand, to recapitulate some sub-lists, especially if they are urgent, is much better than not recapitulating at all. On the other hand, it is much better if you finish your list with all the areas before starting to work with the box.

Whichever method you choose, once you have completed your list, you are ready to go ahead with the next stage: creating the box.

The Importance of the List

One very important thing I want to make clear is that formulating the list is not merely a step preceding the "real work." The list of recapitulation is real work itself, even if you never get the opportunity to do the rest of the work with recapitulation. I do not mean that simply by creating the list you would get the same results or even similar ones as you would by completing the process. But there are many good results that can come from merely creating the list. It is a complete exercise in itself—a more shallow form of recapitulation, but one that is still valuable and useful. The point is that by creating the list, you are making a first approach to your entire life. Working the events inside the box takes the experience to a much deeper and stronger level—and gives a much deeper and stronger result.

I have seen people change a great deal and realize deep insights about what they have been doing in life simply from working on their list. The list is like a map; it gives us the chance to take a wider look at our life. Instead of seeing one event at a time as we do every day, we may look at all the events at the same time. We may see repetitions (i.e., internal routines), tendencies, and so on. We may even notice *dark zones* and track them back to see where and when they originated.

Exercises with the List

Because of its maplike quality, we may practice several exercises that while not a part of the recapitulation technique would nonetheless be able to enrich our experience with the list. For example:

- Copy your *by age stages* list on one big piece of cardboard (you may even attach more than one). Then color the background of each event with a different color: yellow for the energetic events, black for the antienergetic ones, and gray for the ones that are neither energetic nor antienergetic, but neutral.
- Now attach your list to a wall. Stand back a few steps and see what the dominant color is. What color has your life been? In which stages of your life were you living in a more energetic way? Which stages were the darkest ones?
- Notice the dark events. Check to see if they are similar or different. Are they all very different or are many of them just the repetition of the same action in different circumstances?
- Now focus on the darkest areas and try to track back to the origin of those moments of darkness. Be aware that the origin may be a long time ago.

These are just some examples of how your list of events could be used to discover the paths you have been walking throughout your life.

Now going back to the Ten-Steps Technique, you are going to use your list at two different times:

1. At the beginning of the entire process, when you create your list for the first time.
2. In the time just before you enter into your recapitulation box. The list is going to be your daily guide that will help you to choose which events or which parts of your life you are going to recapitulate in that specific session.

Following your list, you will be able to see what parts of your life you have recapitulated already and what others are still pending.

Tips and Hints

- Work on your list in a place where and a moment when you are not going to be disturbed.
- Work with deep concentration; take your time working on your list—it is a ritual time to look into yourself.
- Work in sessions of at least one hour each.
- Try to work with it often enough that you do not lose all connection with the task of remembering in the time between two sessions of work. Because of the risk of losing connection, intensive periods of working on your list are more powerful than many sessions spread over a long period of time.
- If you cannot engage yourself in a nonstop process, then try to work with the list in segments without breaking your connection with each segment until you have finished working with it. Examples of segments might be; childhood or adolescence; partners, and relatives.

8

Step 2: The Recapitulation Box

For several reasons, some people find the idea of the box hard to accept. The ones I have heard the most are:

- The idea of the box is a little bit scary.
- It seems impossible for me to stay "trapped" in a box of wood for a long time.
- I am claustrophobic.
- I wonder if it dangerous.

These and other thoughts bring some people to the big question: Is it possible to recapitulate without using the box?

The answer is simple: Yes, it is possible, but it is much easier to do it with the box for many reasons:

- The box is a place for retreat where you will find solitude, quiet, and darkness, which are ideal conditions for recapitulating. You could use a cave as well, but you probably cannot find caves in the place where you live.

- The box helps you to create a special atmosphere. It is so different from ordinary surroundings that simply by entering into it your body feels that something unusual is going on. This helps to awaken the other side.
- As a ritual element the box helps you focus your attention on the task of recapitulation.
- Each time we practice recapitulation inside the box, the box becomes impregnated with the energy of the special attention we use during recapitulation (second attention). As an object of power, once it's charged with this energy, the box calls forth that special attention each time we enter it.
- When we are in the recapitulation box, our energetic body is a little bit compressed, and this effect of compression helps the body to remember.
- The symbolic sense of the box—its representation of how we are trapped in our personal history, for instance— is very useful for the final rituals of recapitulation, such as when we burn the box as a representation of our will to leave behind the personal history, to be free.

All these elements make recapitulating with the box much easier than without it. Once we have finished the main recapitulation of our life, if we thereafter we want to recapitulate, and our body is familiar enough with the process, we can do so without the box.

Statistically, I have seen many people recapitulating with the box, and I have seen others trying to do it without the box. The results of the people using the box are better, by far. To say it succinctly, you may venture into the task of recapitulating your life without the box, but I highly recommend you use it.

What About the Fears?

Well, I have passed through experiencing the fears, and I have accompanied many others in the same task. The fears are not connected with the real experience of working with the box. The normal initial feeling of fear vanishes once you start your work. Actually, you come to a moment when you find yourself at ease within your box. I have not seen people experiencing claustrophobia inside the box, even if they believe they are claustrophobic. You do not feel trapped because the experience of reliving takes your perception to much more open spaces than the space of your box. Finally, there is no danger at all in recapitulating in a box, as long as you take care to build your box with good air intake.

There are basically only two real fears behind the resistance to recapitulate inside a box:

- The fear of change that your ego feels, because change is the one thing that the ego resists the most.
- The fear of physical work. The fantasy that building a box of wood is very difficult most of the time is just an excuse for our laziness. The truth, as we will see, is that building your box is not difficult at all.

The Building Process

The recapitulation box is a simple rectangular wooden box. One of the long walls of the box should have hinges, so it may be used as a door. You open the door to enter, and you close the door once you are inside.

The size of the box depends on your own size while seated with your legs crossed. For a preliminary idea of how the box looks, see figure 9.

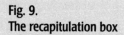

Fig. 9.
The recapitulation box

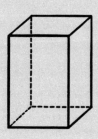

The stages for building the box are these:

1. Finalize the measurements of the box
2. Collect the planks and other materials for the box
3. Assemble the box yourself

Finalizing the Box Measurements

You are going to be seated inside the box, with your back leaning against its wall and your face to the door (the front wall). The idea is that the space should not be too big or too small. The distance between your knees and the side walls should be approximately 3 inches; this should also be the distance between your head and the upper wall. The distance between your knees and feet and the front wall (i.e., the door) should be 5 inches.

All this means is that in order to get the exact measurements, you should measure yourself (with the assistance of somebody else) while you stay seated in a crossed-legged position, with your back leaning against a wall. Following this system, your friend is going to measure the following distances while you stay in position.

Take note of the following measurements:

A = Distance from the wall to the front part of your knees, plus 5 inches

B = Distance from the side part of one of your knees to the side part of the other knee, plus 6 inches (3 inches per side)

C = Distance from the floor to the top of your head, plus 3 inches

Once you have these measurements, you can estimate the size of the planks that you need:

For the floor and the top of the box, you need two planks of A x B
For the side walls of the box, you need two planks of A x C
For the front wall (i.e., the door), you need a plank of B x C
For the rear wall, you need a plank of B x C (½ inch)

The rear-wall plank is a little bit shorter than the one at the front, to create a good air intake. Avoid placing your box flush to a wall, to prevent the air intake from being blocked.

Collecting the Materials

With the proper measurements at hand, you may either buy a big plank and make the cuts yourself or buy the planks already cut to the desired measurements.

We recommend you use recycled wood for ecological reasons. Do not use plastic or metal instead of wood, because the energetic configuration of those materials is not as "friendly" for human beings. Cardboard is not recommended because of its lack of durability.

List of materials

Six planks of the appropriate measurements, all of them ¾ to 1 inch in thickness
1½-inch nails
Two metal hinges with wood screws
Small lock bolt (to lock the door from the inside to prevent the door from being opened accidentally)
8 ounces of wood glue

Tools

Hammer

Screwdriver

Gloves

Assembling the Box

It is fundamental that you assemble your own box. I know it would be very easy to pay a carpenter to assemble your box, but in terms of energy that box would not work the same way.

I am not going to describe here the technical work of assembling the box, because it is such a simple structure that I know you will find the way. If you are not familiar with handling tools at all, then great! The extra effort you will make to figure out how to do it is going to be part of your energetic offering, which at the end is going to create better results.

Actually, the process of assembling the box is very important in terms of the power your recapitulation box is going to have. The main issue is that you should build your box as a ritual. Deep concentration in every single thing you do while you build the box is a requirement. You must not be thinking about anything other than the building of your box for recapitulation.

Establish an internal connection between the past you are trapped in and the box you are building. While you work on making your box, think about your past, your reasons to engage in recapitulation, what areas of your life you need to change. Think about the purpose of your recapitulation. Imagine yourself working inside the box, facing the challenge. Make a commitment to yourself to accomplish the whole process, from the beginning to the end. Think of the freedom you are looking for.

When you build your box, do not do anything else. Do not talk, do not listen to the radio, and do not watch TV. Just keep a silent connection with the box and all that it represents. It is your initial ritual, it is going to happen just once, and it should be done in full awareness.

Choose a proper place to build your box. Usually it is done in the same place where you are going to be recapitulating. The ideal conditions would be a house or cabin surrounded by trees, but any other quiet place will work as well.

Do not put any drawings or designs on the box. It should be simple, plain wood.

How to Use the Box

Once you have the box, you are ready to start your recapitulation.

The place to locate your box should be quiet and dark, so that exterior sources of light do not distract you. It is important that you arrange everything so that no one can interrupt your work or disturb you in any way while you are recapitulating.

Let us say that you have studied your list, so you know what events you are going to recapitulate. You have already done the preparation exercises that will be explained later on. You are ready to enter into your box.

You enter, sit down, and close the door. You remember what you are going to recapitulate or you may even take a look at a small notebook in which you have written down the events you need to remember to recapitulate in that session. A small flashlight may be useful to allow you to read your notes. You will not turn on your flashlight for any other reason, because doing so would cut into your recapitulation work.

So you now know the event you are going to recapitulate, and you begin to perform the starting breath of the recapitulation. . . .

That is how you begin using your box, and you will continue the process there until you finish your session of that day. The more you work in your box, the more it becomes charged with the special attention of your recapitulation. You will feel that you are entering a not-normal space, where everything is related to the not-doing of memory: the recapitulation.

Because of this energetic charge, it is important to prevent sensitive beings, especially pets or children, from entering your box. Once the box is impregnated with the energy of your past experiences, a child or your dog entering there could catch part of this energy, which is often quite heavy. This may result in sickness or "bad luck" for the child or the animal. Your recapitulation box is for you alone, and nobody else should enter it.

Tips and Hints

- You may use a thin cushion to sit on while you are inside the box. If there is cold weather, use a good sweater or a not-too-thick jacket.
- Avoid cushions or jackets that are too thick or any kind of pillow. Besides the fact that those things may reduce the space within your box, they could create the additional problem of making your box too comfortable. A box that is too comfortable is not beneficial to the process—it might lead you to feel sleepy.
- Avoid the temptation of making your box a little bit wider to have a more comfortable space. While some people like to have an apartment-like box, the truth is that without having the sensation of a reduced space, recapitulation work is much more difficult.
- Avoid calling excessive attention to your box and to your recapitulation work in general. Instead of trying to explain how your recapitulation box works, you may simply say that this is the box you use for meditation. Most people would find an explanation like this easier to deal with than "shamanic healing technologies." The point here is to avoid being disturbed by other people's attention to your work.

9

Steps 3 through 8: Inside the Box

I n this chapter we will discuss the core of the whole process of recapitulation. This chapter will answer the main question about the recapitulation technique: How does the process of reliving and healing events take place? How do I do it?

First of all, the process I am going to explain is what you are going to apply to every single event of your list or to each series of interrelated events. This means that while the list and the box are to be created only once, the procedure inside the box is going to be done many times.

Distinction between an event and a series of interrelated events is important in order to avoid confusion. This distinction comes from the fact that it is not easy to determine exactly when one event starts and when it ends. It happens that almost any event could be divided into smaller events. Also, any event could be considered to be part of a bigger event. This is so because in life we are dealing more with process than with single isolated happenings. It is natural that deciding when an event starts and ends is not always easy.

Because of this you should be flexible and trust your own feelings about when you are going to recapitulate one event and when you are going to recapitulate a series of events that are linked together. Don't worry if this sounds a little bit confusing; when you practice this, it will be easier for you to understand. In fact, this is for the whole process in general. You find the answers and the real understanding as you go. For the moment you should know that you have the freedom during the process to be flexible and arrange and choose events in the way you find most convenient for your work.

Now, for you better to understand the process inside the box, here is an outline of what you will do.

Once you have chosen the event to recapitulate, you enter the box and begin a special way of breathing that is named, simply, breathing technique 1. This allows you to achieve concentration and focus in the act of recapitulating. In the next step, you see the event as though you were watching a movie. Then you are inside the movie, reliving the events and the feelings you had during the event. Last, you are out of the event, watching it again, but this time you apply special techniques of breathing to recover your energy or release whatever you need to remove from your self and your life.

Up to this point the movie (i.e., the event) has been played three times: the first time you were a spectator seeing the event from outside. The second time, you were inside the event, reliving. The third time, you were seeing the event again from outside, but this time you were healing the event using your special breathing.

In the next step, you come to decisions that are the conscious changes you are going to make as an expression and reinforcement of the healing you did with your breathing. Finally, you dream yourself accomplishing actions in your real life that correspond to your healing and decision making.

Once you have done this, you have finished the recapitulation of that event or series of events and you are ready to move on to the next one. Just breathe normally and cleanse your mind before starting again. You may start to see the next event with or without the breathing, depending on whether or not you feel you need it. You continue with the next steps as you did before.

This is the outline of the process so far. Now let's examine each step, one by one, using specific examples.

In order to make the process less confusing, I am going to leave for later (chapter 11) the explanation about the specific procedure of how and in what cases to perform each of the special breathing techniques. For the moment, it will be enough to know that there are two main breathing techniques to be used as needed in the moment of energetic restoration. Technique 1 is used to recover lost energy and to start the process in the box. Technique 2 is used to release foreign energy and finish with energetic routines. In chapter 11 we will look at these and other breathing techniques in detail.

Step 3: Starting the Breathing

In this step you enter the box and adopt the posture for recapitulation. Your back is leaning against the wall, your spine is straight, your legs crossed. Some thin people may do it by embracing their legs.

Now close your eyes and start doing breathing technique 1 over and over again, until you feel that your body is ready to start recapitulating. Usually this takes from five to ten minutes, depending on how you feel in that moment and how much practice you have had with this breath. The more you practice, the sooner you will be ready to recapitulate.

Step 4: Seeing the Event

Now you are going to see the event as if you were in a theater. On the screen of your mind, you are watching a movie; the script of the movie is what happened during the event you have chosen to recapitulate. The main actor of the movie is you. You are seeing yourself in that movie. You are seeing your past.

While you watch, try to use your memory in a different way. Pay attention to the details—the surroundings, the objects. *The main thing is to direct attention to the feelings inside the actors.* See their looks and try to feel their hidden thoughts. What is happening on the surface? What is going on inside them? See your own feelings.

Using the example of Mary, let us imagine that now she is recapitulating her life in order to heal what is wrong with her. She is in the box, has started breathing, and is recapitulating that terrible day when her father came home angry and depressed and rejected her violently.

She is seeing little Mary running to look for her father. She is seeing the man pushing the little girl. But now she is seeing not only the crying eyes of the little daughter. She is seeing the pain and confusion in her father's eyes as well. In looking at the event from outside this time, she has a wider vision, and she uses it. This is what I mean by using your memory in a different way. Try to see everything. This step may take from a few minutes to twenty or even thirty minutes, depending on whether you are working with a single event or a series of events. The length of the event itself has an influence as well. In practice, most often this step does not take more than ten minutes.

Once you have seen the whole movie (i.e., when the event reaches an end), you are ready for the next step, the very core of the recapitulation.

Step 5: Reliving the Event

Now the story is going to be played again. But this time you are *inside* the event. You do not see yourself—you see only the people who were with you in that moment. You are living the present, and you are doing the same thing you were doing in the actual event.

You are speaking the same words, you are having the same thoughts, you are feeling the same feelings of that time. It is the here and now. In order to relive and not just remember, you should act the event. Within the limitations of the box space, move your body a little bit, just to feel more what you are living. Say the words you said. Say even what you didn't say in the actual event but what was present in your feelings and thoughts. Do not analyze what is going on. You are there living and feeling, and there is no time or space for anything else other than what you are living and feeling.

The main goal here is to pass from the space of remembering to the space of reliving. Depending on how naturally this process takes place, you may need to do some intensification practices to trigger the bodily process of reliving.

Now, what are we looking for in this step, and what may stop us from getting it? We are trying to relive a past experience, but that goes against our usual perception of time, which is that the past is gone. Therefore, reliving the past is something that our rational mind just cannot accept. The point is, no matter how much this may sound like nonsense, it is what we should do: relive the past.

This is one of the most crucial moments of the whole process of recapitulation. Reliving past events is not easy, but it is crucial that you learn how to do it at the outset. Otherwise, you are going to be hitting the same obstacle again and again.

This is a big challenge because this part of the recapitulation process implies entering into a state of nonordinary reality, which means, among other things, leaving behind the control of the rational mind and surrendering to the experience.

The main problem is that it is difficult to try to do something at the same time your mind is telling you that it is not possible. In other words, you want to relive but you feel stupid trying to do something that you think is impossible. This is the crucial point. In order to get to the other side, where the impossible is possible, you should overcome the common perception that is stopping you. But how do you do this? Well . . . there are techniques, which I will describe here, but you should be aware that there is no technique strong enough to succeed if your inner being is saying no.

One of the common ways in which an internal no may block your advancement is the feeling of resistance to acting in a "ridiculous" way. Let us be very clear: You should abandon your concern about looking ridiculous right now. What you are dealing with in recapitulation is deadly serious, especially if you fail because of such a silly fear. Think about it when you get to the moment of using the following intensification techniques, which are useful to help you cross to the other side (i.e., from remembering to reliving). Now, assuming you have the proper inner attitude (a firm and clear yes in your heart), here are some of the actions you can take to pull yourself into the experience of reliving:

Talk. Really talk instead of just thinking the words. You can start by whispering, then increase the volume gradually to the point of shouting. In your talking, say the words you said in the actual event; say the words you kept hidden in your mind. Confessing them out loud is a very powerful action to trigger the feelings. Express your feelings by verbalizing them. It is interesting—talking is most of the time an action connected to the rational mind. Nevertheless, when you connect talking to pure feeling, talking could be the catalyst for triggering the expression of what has been hidden in the left side.

Say the names. You can repeat continuously the names of the people about whom you are recapitulating. Start whispering a name and gradually increase the volume until you shout the name. Merely by repeating the name you may create a strong energetic and emotional connection to the person and the events related to her or him.

Move your body. Tremble, shake, make sudden short movements, embrace your body, hold a fetus posture, make cradling movements.

Do intense breathing. Short and fast breaths could help you connect with feelings. At the same time, it is important to remember not to do this for long periods of time, because you could get dizzy or even sick to your stomach. Generally, a few minutes will be enough.

Exaggerate. One of the simplest techniques to connect with feelings and reliving is exaggerating what you were doing, feeling, or saying. If you want to connect with fear, but you don't think you can, then pretend that you are acting, but exaggerate, which means you are going to act or express with even more intensity than in the actual event. This overacting has nothing to do with imparting to the events more importance than they actually had. It is merely a way of handling your energy so that you can break the barrier that prevents you from connecting with your bodily memory of the event.

Cry, shout, sing, laugh, growl, howl, moan, groan. Do anything that may help you stop thinking and start feeling. This is the moment to leave behind the ever-present controlling mind.

You are going to use the previous intensification techniques as much as you need them. They are tools. You may use some or all of them according to your needs. Probably at the beginning of your recapitulation work, you are going to need them more. Once you practice and your resistance to reliving the past breaks down, the reliving will come more naturally.

The resistance to reliving could be seen as a dike: Once it gives way, what was behind it flows. The dike could be made of fear to change. Fear to live again the pain of the past is also a common reason for resisting. Some people say, "I don't want to pass through that suffering again. I don't know if I would be able to bear it." This is understandable when people are dealing with recapitulating a deeply painful event. "I have been trying to leave that pain behind. Why should I go back to that suffering again?" they say. The point is that if you feel so much fear and pain simply from by thinking about the event, then the pain has not gone. It is still with you.

If you do not face it now once and for all, that pain will be after you the rest of your life. The more you try to escape from it, the more it will follow you. That is why recapitulating the events that have hurt us is so necessary, even if we should pass through some pain. The reason for going back there is not just for the sake of suffering but instead to heal our selves of that pain. Recapitulation is a continual challenge. As soon as you have succeeded in the challenge of going back and reliving, you will be facing the next challenge: detaching yourself from the pain and having the capacity and courage to jump out of the event and start the healing.

Step 6: Energetic Restoration

In this step you are going to see the event for a third time to start the healing. In a similar way to what you did in step 4, you will see the event from outside. The movie will again be replayed in front of your eyes and this time you will be a detached spectator, but your role will not be passive. Now you are the healer—a cold and focused healer. There is no sorrow in you; there is no self-pity. There is only will and the power to heal.

In order to heal the event, once again you are going to use the special breathing techniques. If you are seeing an event in which you lost energy, you are going to recover it by using breathing technique 1. If you are seeing yourself in an event in which you were impregnated with other people's energy or if you want to release a promise you have been carrying since that event, use breathing technique 2 to release what should not remain in you. If you are seeing an event in which you lost energy and made a negative energetic command, use breathing technique 1 to recover energy and then technique 2 to revoke that promise.

Breathing is a magical act; it keeps us alive. In this step you are going to use the magical power of breathing to restore your energetic body. While you use the appropriate breaths, you should use your *intent* to recover your energy or release what must be let go. This means that there is no question about what you are doing. You just do it. The power of using your will to heal your energetic body comes from a region of your other self that is called the place of no pity. This is a cold and silent space where there are no thoughts, doubts, or self-pity.

To accomplish the healing, you must go back to the experience that needs to be healed. When the moment arrives, be prepared to jump out of the event and start the healing, no matter how intense your reliving is. Do not leave the event before you get to the core of the feelings you felt in that event; stay for a few minutes, and then, when you have touched the bottom, get out of there. Jump out and start the healing.

To be prepared means knowing in advance that sometimes it is not easy at all to jump out of the event. It seems strange, but it is common that the more painful events are the ones that are more difficult to leave because sometimes the entire structure of our ego has been built upon those critical experiences.

Many people see themselves this way: "I am the one who has suffered that pain. I am the man [or the woman] who carries this wound." The hidden fear of our ego could be expressed this way: "If you take away this wound, which has given meaning to my life, who am I going to be then? What am I going to be?" The resistance to change is more prevalent than we would imagine. It is related to that fear of losing the meaning that our past gives us. Maybe it is not a nice past, but it is what nourishes and sustains our ego. Because of this, the ego is deeply attached to it, and we should be ready to overcome that attachment so we can be free and discover that there is much more inside us than the limited possibilities of the ego and its personal history.

I have seen this resistance to getting free from the attachment to painful events in our recapitulation workshops. I have seen people who first resisted entering into the experience of reliving events of intense emotional pain, and then, when they finally were able to enter into the reliving, did not want to get out. They went back to the pain and started crying without restraint—a pure and complete sorrow poured forth like the flowing of a river when the dike finally breaks. That free flowing of grief is the first step to healing the soul and taking away the heavy weight that has been over us for so long. Nevertheless, the complete healing will take place only if we are willing to let the sorrow go away. The more we keep grasping the pain, the more it will hurt us.

I remember a woman grasping her pain and resisting letting it go during the reliving step. She was crying without stopping.

"Come on, now it is time for the healing. It is time for the next step!" I said.

"I can't, I can't. It is too painful!"

"Of course you can. Don't give in to the sorrow! Jump out of the event and start the healing!"

"I can't, I can't!" she insisted.

It was not true that she could not. She just was not ready to release a wound that had been her companion for so long.

Obviously, not all the events in recapitulation are so painful and difficult to pass through. I give this example only because it represents the ones that we need to recapitulate the most and the ones that may be more complicated to handle.

In the case of an event related to happiness, the restoring-energy procedure is just the same. You relive the event, and once you have reached the core, you jump out no matter how pleasant the experience may be. Then the event again from outside and use the appropriate breath. Maybe what you are seeing is the laughter of your childhood. Use breath number one to bring it back.

Step 7: Decision Making

Once you have completed the healing for that event using the breathing techniques, it is time to change your attention and focus on the decision making. It is important to note that the decision making starts in the rational mind but should get to the energetic body. This means that your decision making is going to take place at two levels. One level is your mind. You think and even state out loud your decision, which is what you are deciding to change in your life and in your being. The other level is the energetic command that will replace the former energetic command that was controlling your life until the time when you started to recapitulate.

Let's look at an example. Let us go back with Mary and her recapitulation. She has seen the painful event with her father, she has relived it, and she has seen the event again and used the proper breathing to restore her energetic body. Now what? Decision making.

Remember how much Mary had been suffering from her incapacity to express her feelings? Now she has recapitulated the event when she made the promise or energetic command of never showing her feelings to others. Mary's decision could be something like this:

"From this moment on, I will not hide my feelings anymore, whatever it takes! I will express my feelings whenever I need to! Fear is not going to stop me!"

It is not easy to transmit the intensity and the power of a decision like this. You would need to be Mary after a whole life of suffering from the incapacity to communicate with others, especially with those whom she loved. Imagine her, after thirty years of emotional solitude, shouting from the bottom of her heart her decision as her freedom declaration.

Thus, making the decision is something that you are going to shout inside your box. But shouting your decision in full awareness is just the external part of the feat. You must feel it with all your being, with your whole body. There should not be any space for doubt. The intensity of your feeling and complete conviction is what makes your decision not just a decision but an energetic command.

Step 8: Dreaming Not-Doings

This is your last step inside the box. The two that follow it will take place outside the box.

The not-doings of recapitulation, or liberated actions, are those actions that, before the process of recapitulation, were beyond a person's capabilities due to traumatic events that left damage in the energetic body

In this step, just after decision making, you are going to dream yourself performing actions that were impossible for you in the past. These actions are not compatible with your personal history but are compatible with what you have done in your recapitulation, and this is why we call them not-doings. Another way to say it is that these liberated actions are specific manifestations of your decision making.

In Mary's case, the liberated actions she could dream would be related to the situations in which she had been troubled because of the promise she had been fulfilling. Therefore, she could dream herself telling her relatives the feelings she has always had about them—she might tell her mother how much she has loved her and how much she missed being touched and embraced by her when she was a child. She would dream herself expressing how important her mother was in her life and how difficult it was for her to handle her mother's rejection when she was five years old. She could also tell her that she understands now that her mother didn't meant to hurt her but that it took thirty years to understand that.

She would dream herself telling her former lover how much she loved him and explaining why she could never tell him. She would dream about the people she loves at the present, telling them what she feels. She would imagine phoning some of them who do not live nearby, just to tell them that they are important in her life.

She would dream herself challenging one of the teachers in the school where she works, a woman who spent time spreading gossip about her just for fun. In her dreaming not-doings, Mary would see herself telling the "fucking bitch" that she is tired of supporting in silence all the gossip that has been building around herself and warning this woman about the serious possibility of losing her teeth if the gossiping doesn't stop.

These are just some examples for the dreaming not-doings step. As you can see, while dreaming the liberated actions, you give yourself the freedom to dream anything without worrying if it is appropriate or not, if it is possible or not, or if it is convenient or not. There will be time for those considerations later on. In this step, let your mind and feelings go freely to those things you have always needed to do.

Dreaming liberated actions fulfills two main purposes: first, to test different possibilities, feelings that we might have inside while dreaming ourselves taking such action. By noticing what we feel, we may discover more clearly what our real being truly needs. Second, and more important, we dream this way to open an energetic door to a new time in our life. We are settling the internal conditions for the liberated actions that we will perform in our real life. The dreaming is the powerful first step toward carrying out the not-doings in our everyday life.

Now let's see about those questions that are spinning around in your head: "What do you mean by dreaming the not-doings? Do you mean 'to imagine'? How can we dream at will?"

Well, I could have said "imagine" the not-doings, but what we should do is closer to dreams than to thoughts. What is the main difference between dreams and imagination? They are not that different, except for the fact that when we dream we feel everything as if it were real. Actually, in the dream what happens *is* real. This is why you dream the liberated acts in this step—to achieve this element of reality you *dream on purpose*. What makes you dream and not just imagine is that you feel what you are dreaming. The point is that your purpose is going to come from your heart and not from your mind, which means you are not going to control your dream. Your feeling is going to set the direction and your body is going to do the rest. To say it in a simple way, do as if you were imagining, but feel as if you were dreaming and take the control of the dream out of the rational mind.

Again, it is easier to do this than to understand it.

One final very important task related to your work in the box: Take notes about the decisions you make and the not-doings you dream. This material is going to be essential for the last steps.

10

Steps 9 and 10:
Living Purposefully

Step 9: Accomplishing the Not-Doings
of Recapitulation

Now you have finished your work inside the box. Strictly speaking, you may say you have finished your recapitulation. However, the AVP technique for recapitulation is not yet completed. There are two remaining steps you should undertake.

For the moment, your energetic body is relieved and stronger. Those ugly holes have been filled by the recapitulation. But do not be too confident. That relief, confidence, and extra energy that you feel is just a patch. It may fail if you don't do something about it. What else could we expect? Those holes have been there for so long.

Probably you would have been able to heal those wounds if you had not started with those energy-wasting routines right after you got wounded. But that is not what happened. Instead of a prompt healing, you tried to hide your wounds under energy-wasting routines. The only result was a reinforcement of the holes and energy loss. And this is the way it has been for many years; this is why a patch is not enough. You have healed yourself, but you need to reinforce the healing the same way you reinforced the wounds so many years ago. This is achieved through persistently practicing the liberated acts or not-doings of those energy-wasting routines.

In order to do so, you are going to take some of the liberated actions you dreamed during your recapitulation, though not all of them can be treated in the same manner. On the one hand, some of the not-doings that you dreamed cannot be accomplished with your physical body. For example, in dreaming liberated actions, you have embraced or asked forgiveness of some important people from your past who are not alive anymore. On the other hand, you have dreamed liberated acts that would be possible to accomplish but would not be convenient. For instance, you have acknowledged to your former lover your unconditional love and have told all the truth that you did not tell in the right moment. Now that former love of your life is out of your world. Maybe she is married and is not thinking about you. Even though it would be nice for you to have an understanding with her, that chance has gone. You have done that in your heart and that is enough. Trying to go further and have an actual meeting with her probably would create more problems than the ones you are trying to solve. In such cases, when the person is not in your world anymore, you heal in your heart. And this is possible because he or she is still living inside you.

This turns our attention to the need for balancing with common sense our commitment to accomplishing the not-doings. There are some liberated actions that you have dreamed that you can accomplish only in your feelings (e.g., not-doings with people who have died). There are others that would not be convenient (not-doings with a former partner who is not in your world anymore). Finally, there are others that you may and should do. These are the ones you are going to practice.

Keep following Mary's case. Let's see from all the not-doings that she dreamed which would be the ones that she should accomplish. First, she is not going to look for her former lover in order to try to have an arrangement with him, because that relationship belongs to a time that is completely gone. Second, she is going to face and resolve the problem with the gossipmonger once and for all, but she probably will think carefully of a more tactful way to do it before she acts. And she is going to talk with her parents and friends, expressing openly the feelings she hid for so long.

It should be clear that these are the examples I am imagining for a person like Mary, but this certainly does not mean that these specific examples of which not-doings to pursue and the ways to pursue them are the only valid course of action for everyone. Each person, each circumstance, is different. Therefore, deciding what not-doings you are going to pursue in your life is your responsibility and no one else's.

Now in the same way I emphasize that your selection of not-doings should be balanced with common sense, I also emphasize that you should be demanding with yourself—do not cheat yourself by choosing only "soft" not-doings. Actually, there are no such things as "soft" or "hard" not-doings. But there are false not-doings and real not-doings. Do the real thing, or do nothing at all and resign yourself to live without power. Remember that the not-doings are a challenge, and the bet on the table is your unique life. So you had better not take chances with them.

There is one important thing to be aware of when you are going to accomplish the liberated actions. Pursuing your not-doings is an arrangement that you make with yourself. You are not going to take the liberated actions to change others. You should perform these actions as an expression of your freedom. You are not looking for reward. We could even say that the liberated actions are our free gesture for spirit.

I am mentioning this because I have seen people who, when the moment of taking the liberated actions arrives, unconsciously try to use those actions to buy others' responses. Such is the case if after a life of hating your father you recapitulate your relationship with him, then in the decision making decide to release the rancor. In dreaming the not-doings you see yourself embracing your father. When you finally attempt actually to embrace the man for the first time in your life, he does not respond in the way you expected because he is not used to physical expressions of affection. This causes you to feel disappointed and angry. You think, "What is the use of trying to heal my relationship with him if he is going to continue being the same callous person his whole life?" At this point all your good intentions to heal your life through recapitulation are gone.

Unfortunately, this kind of situation is common in dealing with relatives or partners. We are changing because we are secretly hoping that by doing so we are going to have what we want from others. Big mistake. The liberated actions are a gesture of freedom. You are healing your energetic body. It is *your* freedom that you are using, so you must do it without expecting any reward more than healing your heart and changing yourself. We cannot rule other people's lives using recapitulation or any other means, because ruling other people's lives goes against the most sacred right: the freedom each of us has to do what we want, and what we can, and the freedom to receive the consequences of our actions.

It is true that often when we change, the world around us seems to change as if by magic. Our change gives us new eyes to see the people around us in new ways. I have heard many beautiful stories of love and reconciliation as a consequence of practicing liberated actions. Nevertheless, we should not assume that these results will come about. That such things might happen should not be our motivation for the action; if it does become our impetus, then our quest for freedom becomes conditioned to other people's reactions, and that is nonsense. The healing responsibility is yours, and the results are yours. Do not misunderstand what the real target is.

Step 10: Continuity (the Master's Step)

Once you have accomplished the appropriate not-doings, you will feel the closing of a circle. That circle was opened when decisive events of your life took place, and only now, after so much time and effort, is the circle closed. For the second time after having finished the recapitulation itself, you are going to think the work is over for you. You have completed and closed the circle, and that is often felt as the end of the recapitulation process. For the second time, this impression is wrong. You have not practiced the not-doings for a long enough period of time.

So the question is, for how long should the not-doings continue? How would you know when you do not need them anymore?

The answer is simple. You will never stop practicing the not-doings of your recapitulation. They will disappear by themselves when they become a normal part of what you are and how you live. Since you don't know when that will happen, you should keep practicing them on purpose. That is what you need, that is what you want, and that is what you will do: Practice the liberated acts.

By doing so, you will discover that acting on purpose is the major art in life: the Art of Living Purposefully. The master's step is continuity— continuity now and for the rest of your life, continuity even when the not-doings become a normal part of your life, because then, at that later time, new not-doings already will be challenging you, and you will accept the challenge and keep fighting. You will know then how it is to be a warrior of the Spirit. And you will be happy, because you will know in the secret region of your silent knowledge that the path of the warrior has always been yours.

11

Additional Procedures

Preparatory Exercises

In our workshops, before entering the box to begin recapitulation we complete different exercises to prepare both the physical and the energetic body for the task of recapitulating. Some of the exercises are designed in relation to the area or season of life that is going to be recapitulated in that session. There are exercises related to the prenatal state, infancy, childhood, adolescence, youth, adulthood, and so on. In addition these are useful exercises for friendships, love relationships, sex, work, and many other areas.

The other category of preparatory practices is the nonseason–nonarea-related exercises. They are designed to provoke states of heightened awareness or the connection with powerful fields of energy—especially the Grandfather Fire—that may help us to achieve our goal.

Within this last category I have selected some exercises you may use in order to achieve a more focused and more intense state of attention, so your work inside the box will be more productive.

Regular Physical Exercise

Gymnastics, jogging, and warming-up exercises are very good to do before entering the box. Approximately twenty minutes could be enough, depending on your physical condition. The optimum level of warming up is achieved at the moment when your body just starts to sweat a little bit. At the same time, this level should not be reached too fast. It is much better to move slowly but continuously than to warm up abruptly.

Ritual with Photos

This practice is both a physical warming up and a ritual to push your body to remember.

Required materials: one picture of you (you need not appear alone) from the period of the event you are going to recapitulate, a glass on which to prop the photo, two simple candles, two small plates to put the candles on, matches or a lighter, a tape recorder, and an appropriate tape of drumming.

For this exercise, place your photo over your box, leaning it against a glass or any other object to keep it in a standing position. Place the lit candles, on plates, on each side of the photo (though not too close).

You should be in front of the box, close enough to see the picture while you start to move, perhaps jogging in place. In the background the drumming music should be playing. Instead of the tape recorder, you may also do this exercise with the assistance of a friend who will drum. The main thing is that you use the sound of the drum to connect yourself with the content of the photo through your movement.

As the music continues, you gradually increase your speed and intensity. From the moment of starting very slowly to the moment of picking up speed, when your body begins to sweat, ten to twenty minutes should pass.

While you move, look at the picture and use the drumming to block your thoughts. Try to travel to the reality inside the picture and feel what is in there. When your body is sweating, slow down, decrease your intensity, and then enter the box.

Exercises with the Fire

If you have the chance to have a bonfire, you can empower your recapitulation by asking the fire to be your guide during the whole process. To be effective, this should be done with heart. Do not ask it if you cannot feel it from your heart.

There are several practices you may follow using the fire.

- Light your fire with full respect, feeling the fire as a sacred presence. Join the spirit of the ancient Toltecs and many other indigenous groups, calling the fire Grandfather Fire as a sign of respect and love. Each time you light your fire, talk to him with real words and not just with thoughts. Ask for his company, advice, and protection during your practices.

- Dancing around the fire while drumming music plays could serve both as a warm-up procedure and as a personal ritual of giving your dance to the fire in a sacred offering. The more you stay in the company of the fire, and the more you give your offerings to him, the more the fire will be your company and guide.

- After your dance, sit down before the fire. Tell him: "Grandfather Fire, just before my recapitulation this night, I want to confess how my life has been and what I have felt during . . . [here you mention the period of time or area you are going to recapitulate]." Then you start to open your heart and reveal to the fire what you have lived and what you have felt. You should talk out loud. If you are recapitulating with others, begin with, "Before you and before all my companions here . . ."

The most important part is that you dare to reach and express your feelings. Talking to the fire requires words that come from the heart, not from the mind. The more sincere and the more intimate your confession is, the more powerful your recapitulation will be. Frequency of confession will depend on several factors, such as the frequency of your recapitulation sessions and the clarity of your connection with the fire. If you are recapitulating every night, do it every three days.

The Burning-the-Box Ritual

When you have finished the recapitulation of your life, a ritual representing the moment you are passing through is appropriate. On the last night of your recapitulation, just before dawn, you are going to burn your box.

Deciding when you have finished your process is not an easy matter. Since you will never be able to recapitulate absolutely all the events of your life, but only the meaningful ones, there will always be the possibility of recapitulating in more detail. You may even spend the rest of your life trying to achieve a more thorough practice. Of course, that is not the idea.

What you need to accomplish is the general recapitulation of your entire life. This means having recapitulated the main issues related to important relationships you have had in your life. Deciding when you have done so is necessarily a personal decision. You are going to do your best to get a balanced result (not too much, not too little), and still there is no way to be absolutely sure that your decision about when you have finished was correct. Don't worry; that's the way it is, not only in recapitulation but also in life in general.

We can do our best, but the mind is going to be there asking, "Are you sure you did it well? Are you sure that was the real thing? Are you sure you are not deceiving yourself?" There is no way to give a definitive answer to such questions. It is merely the mind asking the mind. The bottom line is that there is no way for the mind to completely satisfy the mind.

Fortunately, the new Toltec warriors know that all human beings have the heart to face those unsolvable mysteries. Some indigenous peoples are used to saying that the real thoughts may come only from the heart. It is not possible to define what the heart is, but it is there anyway. All we can do is try to do our best and ask our heart, "Are you satisfied?" A feeling of contentment and satisfaction will mean yes. A feeling of dissatisfaction will simply mean no. In the middle of the mystery, we will make our decision, and there is no way to guarantee the victory. That is why we are warriors.

But let's say our heart says, "Yes, I have finished my recapitulation." During the last night of your process, this is what you will do. You will leave for this last night some meaningful events that are pending. This night you will not sleep. Keep recapitulating until two hours before dawn. Get out of your box and look at it for the last time. That box represents your past and all you have been until that moment; you are about to cross a threshold—once you cross it, nothing will be the same. You will not be the same.

You will disassemble your box with care. What you are disassembling is the structure of your old ego, which is about to die. While you do this, think of the life you are leaving behind. Using tools, break the planks into pieces that you can burn in a bonfire. Obviously, the care you will put into this work also means you are doing it in such a way as not to injure yourself.

Next you go to the fire. Thank Grandfather Fire for his company and guidance. Tell him how you feel on this last magical night, just before the dawn of your new life. One by one throw into the fire the pieces of your recapitulation box; you can even shout the decisions you have made during the recapitulation. See your old energy-wasting routines burning in the flames. Your resentments are there, all the things that should die so you really can live!

After throwing the pieces of your box—the pieces of your past—into the fire, the last thing you will do just before dawn is dance before the fire for the last time in your recapitulation adventure. Accompanied by the sound of drumming, express through your dance all the efforts and struggles you have passed through as you searched for your freedom. With your dance say goodbye to your old self and to your personal history. You will be reborn, but this time, for the first time in your life, *you* will choose how to be and how to live.

When the first rays of the sun touch the world, see a line crossing the fire in front of you. That is the boundary of personal history. Concentrate all your energy, feelings, and thoughts in a final action: Run and cross that boundary toward your freedom. You can jump over the fire or cross the line beside him. However you do it, put your whole heart into the action. Shout your gesture to the universe: *I am free!*

The light of the new day will be your baptism; life will be waiting for you. Go ahead, because there is no time to waste.

Activities to Balance Recapitulation Effects

During the time of recapitulation, you will notice several effects in your life. As with any change, these effects will require a period of time and even a strategy for you to adapt to and properly handle them.

The changes resulting from recapitulation are, in general, positive. Extra energy, the chance to break old energy-wasting routines, and the opportunity to choose—on purpose—new ways to respond to the challenges of your life are just some of the most valuable. Some of the changes are going to happen during your recapitulation and others will come later.

The work of recapitulation leads your being to a new time. Changing is an intrinsic part of the process. Nevertheless, you should know that in doing recapitulation you are entering into a battle between two opposite impulses present inside you: the impulse to change and the impulse to remain the same. On the one hand, your being of energy is, as are the rest of the fields of energy in the universe, naturally oriented to change and movement. On the other hand, your ego's everyday work is to try to keep and reinforce all the structure of thoughts and routines on which it is based.

Because of this, certain routines of your ego are going to feel threatened. The part of you that does not want to change is going to try to stop your work in recapitulation, sometimes making you think you are very tired. In addition, short periods of fear, worry, or desperation may occur. As a general rule, those thoughts will come sooner or later. But also as a general rule, the little voice in your head is going to be lying. Do not give up—instead of giving up and thinking thoughts of worry, pursue activities that help you to cleanse your mind and spirit.

Not only during the recapitulation but after the recapitulation as well, your old ego is going to try to pull you back to the old ways that were so comfortable. The more you keep giving attention to that little voice, the more the ego and its driving force, the fear, are going to be strengthened. You should be ready to resist their attack. At the same time, if you have a good strategy, those attacks are not a big deal. Again, what you need is to include some activities in your life that pull your attention to the proper side: your luminous being.

The kinds of activities I am talking about should play the role of balancing you in relation to the possible temporary attacks of your old ego. If you practice them, the frequency and intensity of those attacks are going to decrease or even disappear. These activities could be of different varieties. The following suggestions will give you some useful ideas to start with.

Outdoor Activities

This is the first and main item you should include in your list of activities complementary to the recapitulation. Any kind of healthy activity in nature is going to have a very beneficial influence on you. The healing effect of interacting with nature comes from the fact that nature does not express self-importance as we do. Nature reflects the Great Spirit; it is as simple as that. The more we respectfully interact with nature, the more we are going to be interacting with the Great Spirit. When they are close enough, fields of energy interact with and influence each other. Being with nature is going to affect positively your energetic body. Your interaction can take many different forms, such as:

- Long, silent walks
- Tree-climbing, being very careful and loving with both the tree and yourself

- Hiking hills or mountains
- Engaging in all kinds of nature-friendly sports
- Playing games with your friends
- Painting in the woods—maybe landscapes
- Silently observing of nature, trying to learn and imitate some of its ways
- Practicing some personal ritual in nature that helps you balance your energy
- Dancing before the fire, making offerings, meditating, doing tai chi, creating music or poems

Feel free to design your own activities as well.

Exercises in the City

Not only in the country can you engage in activities to balance your energy in relation to the effects of recapitulation. If you notice that heavy thoughts often appear, you can do something about them even in the city. Seek activities with no other purpose but to enjoy yourself:

- Maybe you can go to that restaurant that you like so much, but which you don't visit often because it's expensive.
- Spend money on something that you really like.
- Go back to the gym you have left for so long and take care of your body again.
- Visit that old friend or relative whose company is so good for you but whom you haven't visited recently because you've had no time.
- If you go to the movies, choose a film that will be good for your spirit.
- Do not spend your time watching TV news or talking with people who always dwell on disasters or worries.
- Seek the company of children and play with them.
- Do something good for others, just for the sake of doing it.

- Set aside specific periods of time (however many hours per day or per week) to practice the golden rule of taking care of your energy: Do not criticize, do not judge, and do not complain.

Now you have some examples of what to do to balance the effects of recapitulation. If you include some of them in your strategy, the fear-inspiring game of the ego is not going to give you big problems. Remember to make time for these balancing activities both during and after the recapitulation process.

Recapitulation Technique for Single Events

Recapitulation is a useful technique to restore damage to or loss of internal balance, even if the damage is small or recent. Actually, it is much better to recapitulate an event when the effects of that event are still fresh than to wait until a wound becomes serious. Because of this, the practice of recapitulation is going to remain a powerful healing technique even after we have finished the recapitulation of our entire life.

When something that puts our energy out of balance happens, it is helpful to recapitulate that event. Doing so will enable you not only to re-balance your energy more easily but also to handle the external results of that experience in a healthier way. Thus, you can prevent creating new energetic wounds in your energetic body.

A simple example of this could be when you have a serious fight with a person whom you love. Maybe you hurt that person or you feel hurt by him or her. Recapitulating that event is going to provide a deeper realization of what happened during the event, which will cause you to stop losing energy, and this way you will be in much better condition to have a healing understanding with that person.

For this kind of situation or others that call for the recapitulation of single events, we have a special technique. You do not have your box for recapitulation, and it would be nonsense to build a new box for each new antienergetic exchange you may have.

For this technique, choose a quiet place. It is preferable although not essential that the place be dark so that you may concentrate easily. Sit down in a chair with your back against the chair's back; your spine should be straight. You may also sit on the floor, cross-legged, with your back against a wall. (A chair or wall is not necessary if you are accustomed to sitting down with your spine straight while leaning your back against something.)

Now that you are located in the appropriate place and time, just follow the steps listed here:

1. Begin circular breathing (breathing technique 4, described below) and continue for some minutes while you try to travel back to the event. As you move your head, very slowly at the beginning and then a little bit faster, see images related to the event and the people involved passing beside you at great speed, like moving pictures on the wall of a tunnel you are entering. Keep doing this until you feel an internal connection with the feelings of that event.

2. Stop the circular breathing and begin following steps 4 through 8 of the Ten-Step Technique. When you get to step 6 (i.e., energetic restoration), you may work with breathing techniques 1 and 2 or with sweeping breathing (breathing technique 3, described below).

3. After your recapitulation, follow the normal sequence of not-doings and continuity, as you would in general recapitulation.

Breathing Techniques

Now it is time to learn exactly how to perform the special breathing techniques for recapitulation. It is important to understand that these techniques should be used only for recapitulation; to use them otherwise will cause them to lose part of their power, and the results will be significantly diminished.

I have mentioned two main techniques before—technique 1 and technique 2, related to recovering and releasing, respectively. Now we will discuss these main techniques, together with others that are very useful. Note that all the breathing should be done with the eyes closed and, except for the circular breathing, should be done through the nose.

Breathing Technique 1

Name: While we call this technique 1, it is also known as inhalation, because that is what is emphasized.

When used: It is used in the moment right after entering the box (step 3) as initial breathing and during the restoration phase (step 6) when required.

Purpose: (1) The breathing is to provide the focus and state of attention appropriate for recapitulation. (2) In the restoration phase it is used to recover lost energy or to recover a quality of our being that we lost in the past (e.g., joy, confidence).

Duration: As required, according to your own feeling.

Procedure: Before starting the breathing, look straight ahead and expel all the air in your lungs. Turn your head to face to the right; then, while you turn your head to face left, inhale, coordinating your inhalation with the movement so that by the time you are facing fully to the left, your lungs and abdomen are full. Move your head to face straight ahead again, holding your breath. Exhale, when you are looking straight ahead again, just as you did at the beginning. Repeat these steps as long as your process requires them.

Figure 10 shows the movements described in the preceding paragraph (the person is seen from above).

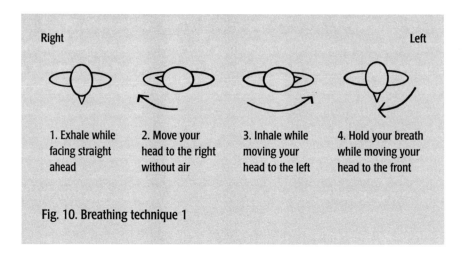

Right   Left

1. Exhale while facing straight ahead

2. Move your head to the right without air

3. Inhale while moving your head to the left

4. Hold your breath while moving your head to the front

Fig. 10. Breathing technique 1

Breathing Technique 2

Name: While we call this technique 2, it is also known as exhalation, because that is what is emphasized.

When used: It is used during the restoration phase (step 6) when required.

Purpose: It is used for several purposes: (1) to release foreign energy, which we received from another person in the past (e.g., parents, former lovers) and which we experience as feelings, recurrent thoughts, or behaviors that do not belong to us; (2) to finish with promises or energetic commands that are blocking our freedom; (3) to let go of ways of behavior or emotional routines (fear of something, rancor, distrust; (4) to say goodbye and break free from people who left but whose leaving we never accepted.

Duration: As required, according to your own feeling.

Procedure: You begin by facing straight ahead and inhaling. While holding your breath, with your lungs and abdomen full of air, turn your head to the left. Then, while you turn your head to face the right, exhale slowly, coordinating your exhalation with the movement so that by the time you are facing fully to the right, your lungs are empty. Now, with no air, turn your head to face straight ahead, then start the whole process again, continuing for as long as you need to. (See figure 11.)

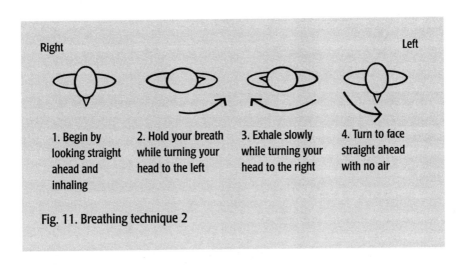

Right   Left

1. Begin by looking straight ahead and inhaling

2. Hold your breath while turning your head to the left

3. Exhale slowly while turning your head to the right

4. Turn to face straight ahead with no air

Fig. 11. Breathing technique 2

Breathing Technique 3

Name: This is called the sweeping breath and is a summary of the previous two breathing techniques. It is sometimes called emergency breathing because you use it when restoration is required and you are not clear which breathing technique is the one you need in that moment.

When used: It is used during the restoration phase (step 6). Its use is optional, because this breath is a substitution for techniques 1 and 2. A simple example of when its use is appropriate would be when you are dealing with an event during which you lost a great deal of energy that you need to recover, and you've also made a promise that you need to release. Here you may use the sweeping breath in substitution for the much more refined procedure of using first breathing technique 1 to recover the energy and then breathing technique 2 to release the promise.*

Purpose: It is used for precisely the same purposes as breathing techniques 1 and 2.

Duration: As required, according to your own feeling.

Procedure: You begin by facing to the right. First, inhale at the same time you are turning toward the left, then exhale while you turn back to the right, and so on.
(See figure 12.)

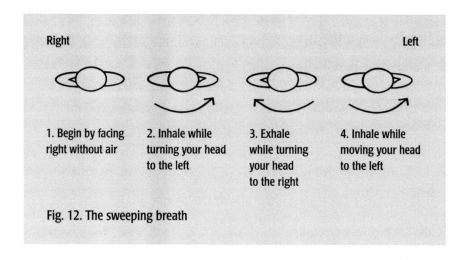

Fig. 12. The sweeping breath

*I prefer to use breathing techniques 1 and 2 instead of summarizing them in the sweeping breath, because I have found the handling of energy more precise when the moment of recovering and the moment of release are separated. It is also true, however, that from a practical point of view this summary breathing is a useful tool.

Breathing Technique 4

Name: This technique is called circular breathing.

When used: It is used to start the recapitulation of single events or a series of events within isolated recapitulation sessions when the box is not employed. It is generally used by people who have finished the recapitulation of their entire life but also want to recapitulate meaningful events that have taken place since.

Purpose: Its purpose is to provide a deep level of concentration and to focus the body memory when not using the recapitulation box.

Duration: As required, according to your own feeling. It is important not to exceed the required duration; otherwise, dizziness or nausea may occur.

Procedure: This breathing should be done while moving your head in a circular way. Start by facing straight ahead with your head tilted close to your right shoulder. Then begin making a slow circular movement upward, toward your left shoulder. While you do this, inhale through your nose. Once you get to your left shoulder, without stopping continue your circular movement, this time downward and toward your right shoulder. While you do this, exhale through your mouth, very softly.

This is the only recapitulation breathing technique that includes breathing through the mouth. This exhalation through the mouth should resemble the gesture of blowing into a balloon in a very soft way. At the beginning your movements should be very slow. As you continue, your circular movement will become a little bit faster and then faster still. However, your movements should not be so fast that they become violent.

Do this technique for two to five minutes, depending on how you feel. (See figure 13.)

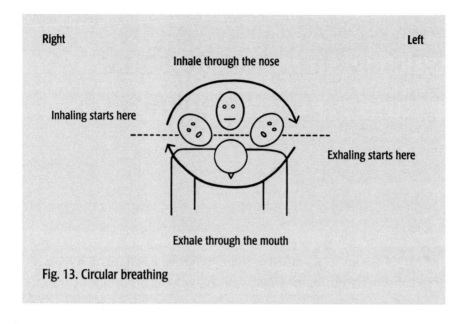

Fig. 13. Circular breathing

12

Designing Your Personal Program of Recapitulation

We are getting to the end of this book. Our only pending issue is how you are going to organize your own recapitulation program in terms of space and time. This is an area in which the lack of specific instructions could stop novice practitioners before they start.

Place and Time

I am going to tell you the *ideal* conditions for recapitulating, but please do not think that if you are not able to reach all the ideal conditions, you are not going to be able to do the recapitulation. Actually, it is rare that people have *all* the ideal conditions that are mentioned in the following list:

- Quiet and solitude are important. Your recapitulation is not going to be possible if there is a lot of noise around or if someone opens the door of your box or calls you out for some reason.
- A house, cabin, attic, basement, or warehouse may work. The idea is not to recapitulate outdoors to protect you and your box from inclement weather. The ideal place would be a cabin in the woods.

- It is not essential, but trees are the most suitable company for somebody engaged in recapitulation. They are protective and helpful to human beings. For reasons beyond our understanding, their energetic configuration and ours have affinity.
- If you have a choice, mountains or hills are better than flat open regions. Unless you live by the ocean and are used to the energy of the sea, do not recapitulate too close to the beach, because the attraction of ocean energy is so strong that entering into the second attention may be a little bit more difficult.
- The best time for recapitulation is when other people are sleeping.
- It is better to have your box in the same place than to move it continually. However, if you want to take your box with you during your vacations for intensive recapitulation, it is all right to move it.

Timing of Your Recapitulation Sessions

Now for a big question: How much time are you going to spend in the whole recapitulation process? Well, the answer is not easy, because there are many affecting factors. Some of them are related to you as an individual, such as how long you have lived, how many important events of your life should be recapitulated, and how much time you need to recapitulate each event or series of events.

But what will affect the time you require to complete your recapitulation are the frequency and duration of your recapitulation sessions. There is no rule in terms of the length of time that everybody should use. That is a personal decision related to your preference and availability of time. Furthermore, there are a few things you should know in advance to help you make your decision.

Intensity multiplies the achievements. In other words, it is more productive to spend one hundred hours distributed over twelve consecutive nights of recapitulation than to expend one hundred fifty hours in six months of three-hour sessions twice a week. This is because once your body starts to recapitulate, the body memory of the experience is still going to be fresh for the next session.

Also, when you recapitulate for two hours and then wait days before your next two-hour session, your body needs time at the beginning of your two hours just to "warm up the motor"; no sooner are you ready to work than it is time to finish.

Another aspect of the same issue is that when you recapitulate frequently enough, the recapitulation becomes the most important thing you are doing in that period of your life. It means you have a strong commitment, and a strong commitment always helps to improve results. When you recapitulate now and then, however, the force of everyday issues may easily overwhelm your process.

Following these premises, our annual AVP workshop to recapitulate in boxes lasts from fourteen to twenty-one nights, with recapitulation continuing through the night. We start with the preparation exercises at 9:00 P.M., enter the boxes at 10:00 P.M., have a half-hour break for sharing in teams or doing another exercise at 2:00 A.M., and then continue working in the box until 6:00 or 7:00 A.M.

I know this may seem like an extreme timetable, but it is not—it is simply practical. Some of the participants sleep for a few hours during the day, but many others do not. They just go to work during the day and return to recapitulate during the night. This is possible because, even though you are not spending the night sleeping as you normally do, your lack of sleep is balanced with the energy you recover and the energy-wasting routines that you stop. This has been my experience in more than thirteen years of work with groups and participants worldwide.

With this information in mind, you can make your own plan. Additionally, find in the following list a series of models of different programs of recapitulation to provide you with an idea of how other people have solved the matter of frequency and length of recapitulation sessions.

- If you have vacations of two to four weeks or you have the chance to spend every night recapitulating, taking some rest during the day for that period of time, then you may undertake a really intensive period of recapitulation. Build your box during the day before the first night; this would allow you to start in the box that same night.
- In this kind of superintensive model, it is useful to work based on the different stages of your life—old age, maturity, adulthood, youth, adolescence, childhood, infancy, and the prenatal state. You can give, let's say, an average of two or three nights per stage, depending on how many people and events you have in each stage. Later on in this chapter, I will talk about how to distribute the events throughout the nights of recapitulation.
- Another possible scenario: You might take off two days from your work along with a weekend, so you could work in periods of four days. During those periods of time you could address specific areas from your list or relationships of certain kinds. Try to finish one area in each of these four-day periods.
- You may do intensive recapitulation sessions several weekends in a row, trying to use the whole weekend and spending as much time as you can recapitulating during both the day and the night. In this kind of program, it is more convenient to work on specific themes or people, instead of working based on life stages.
- You can choose from one to three weekly sessions of two to four hours each, and maybe add another session at one point during the weekend. This certainly requires more time to finish the entire process, but it would work. With this nonintensive system, I suggest spending from three hundred to five hundred hours of effective work inside the box. This would take approximately a year—maybe less, maybe more, depending on your specific circumstances.

As you can see, the program of recapitulation can be organized in very different ways. The examples I provide here and even the number of hours spent inside the box are very, very general ideas based on what we have seen in our years of practice. But in talking about a program design, we should balance those comments and examples with the fact that recapitulation is something that our body does; therefore, every single case will be different. This means that as long as you have a real commitment to the work, you can trust your heart in terms of how much will be necessary to accomplish the process.

Organizing Your List

Once you have decided how often and for how long you are going to have your recapitulation sessions, what you should do next is organize your list of events. There are three main stages in the process of organizing your list.

The First Stage

In this stage you will be selecting the most meaningful relationships and events to make a new list containing only the main events. We are going to call this new list *the list for the box*. It is a shorter list, containing only the more significant events that outlined your life.

Certainly, I could have requested from the beginning that you write down only these main events on the list. The reason for not having done so is that the work on the first list should be done thoroughly, in order to help you to remember more and more and to connect with the feelings associated with the events. Nevertheless, you do not need to recapitulate every single small event from that list inside the box. It would be almost never-ending work, and you need to have results soon enough to still have time to live the new life you are looking for.

For instance, in our intensive recapitulation workshops people should have their list for the box already completed at the beginning. The number of events on it may vary a great deal, depending on how thoroughly each person has worked on his or her list. Numbers go from one thousand to twenty thousand events. Let's say that between two thousand and three thousand is the most common. Now, after fourteen nights, recapitulating all night long, on their list for the box they end up with around five hundred events. Let me explain what I mean by "series of events."

In the practice, when you are recapitulating events, it is very common that they do not come as isolated incidents but are associated with other events from the same relationship or period. In accordance with the feeling of the moment, you may group some of them to be recapitulated at once. As long as you don't do it too often, this option is only natural and helps you make the large number of events on your list more manageable.

Finally, a word about the first big list you generated: It's important to note that all the remembering of small events that are not going to be present on your final list for the box was not useless. All the work you did in registering and selecting them has given you valuable insights and will provide you with the deeper connection with your past that you need in order to do your work inside the box.

The Second Stage

The next stage in organizing your list is deciding the criteria to be used in distributing your events over your sessions. This means deciding if you are going to organize your recapitulation based on the stages of your life (maturity, adulthood, youth), types of relationships (relatives, partners, friends), areas of your life (home, work, schools), or some other.

When you are deciding what criteria you are going to use, take into account the kind of program you will have in terms of frequency and duration of the sessions (intensive, weekends, weekly sessions—see the discussion of timing and frequency earlier in this chapter). Also take into account your personal needs.

Once you are clear about the criteria you will follow to organize the events, decide which category of events you are going to recapitulate first and which category is going to be recapitulated at the end. The recommendation here is to recapitulate what is more present in the current stage of your life first, and then keep going back in time with subsequent stages or themes.

Now relocate the events on your list for the box in accordance with the criteria and order you have chosen to recapitulate them. This means that you will put at the top of your list the events that you are going to recapitulate in the first session, while the ones you are going to recapitulate in the last session will be located at the end of your list.

The Third Stage

The final stage of organizing your list for the box consists of making an equitable distribution of the listed events for all the sessions you are going to have. The idea is that in all of them you should have an equal number of events to recapitulate. Obviously, this may vary depending on how things go inside the box while you work with the events. Some of them will require more time and others less. Anyway, having that initial distribution will help you avoid having too few events in the initial sessions and too many in the last ones.

For example, if you have five hundred events or series of events to be recapitulated in fourteen nights, you will have slightly fewer than thirty-six events per night. Of course, you can do, let's say, thirty one night, forty another night, and so on. It is okay to adjust as you go through the process.

After dividing your list for the box in this way, mark the first thirty-six events on the top of your list "Session (or night) 1," then "Session 2" for the following thirty-six, and so on.

In addition to this, mark in some way those events that are really the most important from your list of thirty-six, so you can keep an eye on them to prevent them from missing out on recapitulation because you run out of time.

The comments and examples I have presented in this section are primarily related to an intensive program of recapitulation. It would take too long here to explain how to organize the list for the box for each possible model of the recapitulation program. So if your program is not going to be as intensive, proceed in a way similar to the one described here but adapt everything to your kind of program and number of sessions.

One additional piece of information that may be helpful for you to know when you design your personal program is the average time that you will need to recapitulate each event. Coming from both my personal and group experiences, I would say that each event or series of events is recapitulated in periods of time that may vary from five to thirty minutes. The average seems to be between ten and fifteen minutes. It should be clear that each experience and person is different, and these are simply approximations.

Final Tips and Hints

I can add tips and suggestions for dealing with only the kinds of problems and doubts I have seen people experiencing throughout thirteen years of working with recapitulation groups.

From the Present to the Past or from the Past to the Present?

Organizing from the present to the past the names of the people on your list or the themes you are going to recapitulate does not mean that you have to recapitulate the events associated with them in this order. Let's say you are going to recapitulate the people of your present life. You can recapitulate the events associated with them, starting from the time when you first met them and finishing with the most recent events you lived with them. But you have the *option* of starting with the most recent events and finishing with the earliest ones, if you feel that doing so would work better for you.

About Distraction while Recapitulating

When you are recapitulating, it is common that some other thoughts or events (i.e., different from the ones you are trying to recapitulate) may attract your attention. Sometimes people become confused because they don't know whether or not it is correct to stop trying to recapitulate the original event, and instead process the event that appears unexpectedly.

There is no one correct solution for this problem. While sometimes it is good to follow the new event, other times it may not be. It depends on the origin of this new event.

If the emerging event has to do with an authentic request from your energetic body, which is showing you the inner need to recapitulate that event, you should follow the feeling instead of pursuing what is on your agenda. On the other hand, if the emerging event is just a trick of your ego to distract you or even just the consequence of your lack of training in keeping your attention focused, make an effort to recover concentration and keep going with the original event.

The big problem, of course, is how to determine whether the emerging event comes from a distraction of your rational mind or from your energetic body. No easy solution, my friend. Just follow your feeling, and try to do your best.

It should be clear that recapitulation is a formal and accurate procedure only on paper. In a real situation it is something that our body does while we try to organize, provoke, and direct what our body is doing. The bottom line is that the energetic body has the control, and we should surrender to its demands. Actually, the only purpose of the energetic body is to follow the healing process. The energy body wants its energy back. Therefore, it is okay to trust its request. At the same time, we should balance this trust in the energetic body (left side) with a sober and disciplined organization from our normal awareness (right side). In other words, too much spontaneity would be as wrong as too much rigidity.

In the end, no matter what you decide to do, trust your decision. That is the warrior's way; maybe you were right, maybe you were wrong. However it is, that unique and personal decision in your heart was all that you had. Nobody could demand anything else from you.

How Deep Should the Recapitulation Be to Have Some Value?

Every single moment of recapitulation is valuable, no matter how deep or how superficial it may be. The range of your recapitulation experiences may go from a deep, deep state of nonordinary reality, with intense reliving, cathartic flowing of repressed feelings, and so forth, to the almost ordinary remembering of the event. Usually, we have a tendency to think that the events recapitulated in deep states of reliving (left-side awareness) have all the value, while the ones recapitulated in more superficial states of awareness lack any value. That conception is wrong.

That is what I thought at the beginning of my research about recapitulation, and that misconception created a lot of frustration and a tendency to interrupt the work. We didn't know what to do in those moments when we were trying to recapitulate an event without being able to reach what we thought was the appropriate "depth."

One extra problem arising from this misconception was the difficulty of having to decide while we were in the box exactly what it was we were doing. Questions such as, "What am I doing? Is this real recapitulation or just normal remembering?" were often troubling our minds.

In the end, this confusion was related to the same problem that took us some years to solve: We were too focused on the left side and trying to do everything from there. When we discovered the secret of the *two sides of recapitulation* (tonal and nagual), everything suddenly became clear—the ordinary memories should be part of the recapitulation process, just as other right-side elements are necessary to have an integral process of healing. Now, before finishing the answer to the question about "deep" recapitulation vs. "superficial" recapitulation, let's see again the table of the elements of recapitulation, to make this matter clear:

Elements of Recapitulation

Left Side—Nagual—Energetic Body

The recapitulation box

Body memories

Breathing techniques

Energetic command

Rituals

Energetic body restoration

Right Side—Tonal—Normal Awareness

List of events

Ordinary memories

Choosing purposeful acts

Decision making

Talking about the process (feedback)

Carrying out purposeful acts

You will notice that there are as many right-side elements as left-side elements. You can recognize and understand most elements of the Ten-Step Technique that have been explained before in this book. Additionally, there are two elements that have not been explained so far: the role of ordinary memories in the process and "talking about the process." Let's focus on the first one.

Ordinary memories are part of the right-side elements of the recapitulation process just as body memories are part of the left-side elements. Imagine a line. At one end we have the most superficial ordinary memory.

At the other end we have the deepest nonordinary-reality body memory. (See figure 13.)

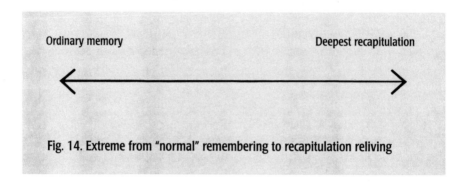

Ordinary memory   Deepest recapitulation

Fig. 14. Extreme from "normal" remembering to recapitulation reliving

When we are recapitulating, we are always at some point between the two ends, though it is not possible to say at which point at any given moment—we feel what is going on, not knowing where to locate our experience in relation to the two ends.

Now, the point is that recapitulation is similar to dreaming—and there is a fine distinction between dream awareness and being-awake awareness. We can see this in figure 14:

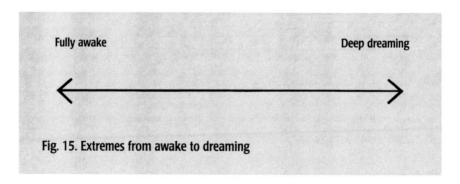

Fully awake   Deep dreaming

Fig. 15. Extremes from awake to dreaming

As we can see in the diagram, there are many points in between dreaming and being awake, such as the meditation state, also known as alpha in terms of brain frequency level of this state. When we are dreaming, we are traveling from the most superficial states of being asleep to the deepest ones, which is when dreams take place. Additionally, dreams could be deeper or less deep, depending on the frequency of where we are when we are experience them. Figure 15 shows this.

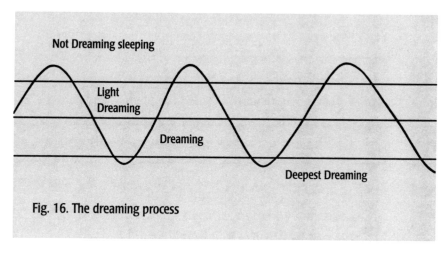

Not Dreaming sleeping

Light
Dreaming

Dreaming

Deepest Dreaming

Fig. 16. The dreaming process

In figure 15 you can see that while you are sleeping you go back and forth from very deep states to not-so-deep states. The same happens with the recapitulation process—your awareness fluctuates from the deep recapitulation states to near-to-ordinary-memory states, which is completely normal. (See figure 16.)

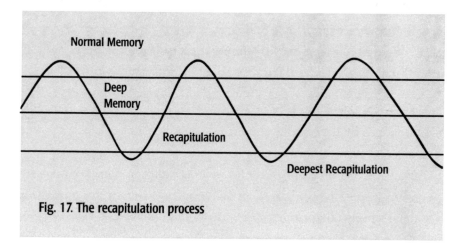

Normal Memory

Deep
Memory

Recapitulation

Deepest Recapitulation

Fig. 17. The recapitulation process

But what should you do when you are recapitulating in a near-to-ordinary-memory state? Well, you will do just the same as when you are experiencing deep recapitulation. The warrior's rule is to use whatever is at hand to accomplish your task. This means you are going to apply the Ten-Steps Technique for all the events, no matter what your state may be.

Do not worry; go as deep as you can and then, without being anxious about how deep you are, follow the procedure of the Ten-Steps Technique. Of course, it is helpful when you can work at a very deep level, but you cannot stay at this level all the time. Fluctuations from the left side to the right side and vice versa are part of recapitulation in the same way that fluctuations are part of dreaming. And this is why *ordinary memories* are included as one of the right-side elements of the recapitulation process. In summary, there is no reason to reject these memories—instead, use them as a part of your recapitulation.

Talking about Recapitulation?

The only remaining element of the recapitulation process that has not been explained so far is *talking about the process,* or feedback. Should we talk with other people about the process? Most of the time the answer is simply no. The reason for this is that by talking to others you would be calling their attention, thoughts, and opinions into part of the process, and most of the time that would interfere with your task. On the one hand, it is not easy to make others understand why you are involved in such a weird thing as spending your time in a box. On the other hand, what you are looking for is very elusive and difficult to understand, even for you.

There are a few exceptions when it is appropriate to talk with others about your recapitulation. One such instance is when you talk with people you are recapitulating about. You can do that if you feel it helps you to gain a deeper connection and only if you are sure that talking to them will not create an emotional problem for you. You should not, however, explain what you are doing to them or reveal that you are recapitulating them but simply talk in a casual way. It should remain low-key.

Exception number two is when you have the chance to share the recapitulation process with other people who would be properly your companions in battle. This happens when two or more people decide to recapitulate together. In this case they may have short periods of feedback where they share with each other what is going on with their experience. This kind of sharing is helpful in reinforcing the focus on the task and putting any stuck energy in motion.

Am I Allowed to Sleep during Recapitulation?

A very direct answer is required for this question: You are not allowed to sleep during recapitulation—if you do it on purpose. But if you fall asleep involuntarily while recapitulating, sleeping is okay. During the process of recapitulation, your state of awareness may change a great deal, which means that you pass through very different modes of perception when you cannot say if you are dreaming, half awake, or awake. Your reality changes, and you should not try to determine exactly whether you are asleep, awake, or something in between. You should just go ahead with the process, no matter what state you are passing through. Actually, some of the most significant moments of recapitulation take place in the dreaming state, which means you are asleep but are continuing with the recapitulation process. The point is that you keep acting with the aim of recapitulating. However, when you say, "Well, it's late; I'm going to sleep," you are breaking the continuity of the work. Do not do this.

What Happens If You Remember More Important Events after Finishing the List?

That is a very common situation. People remember more events as they keep working with recapitulation. Sometimes it happens while you are in the box; sometimes it happens when you are doing something else. Incorporating these events into your work process is certainly helpful, especially when the events that come to your attention have been an important influence on your life.

In the case of these events coming to you while you are recapitulating something else, first follow my recommendations for dealing with distracting thoughts or digressions. If the event is a real pending issue, you should choose between working with that event at that moment or leaving it for later. If you feel the event is important and it arrives by itself, then take a chance and follow it right away. Sometimes an "urgent" event shows up unexpectedly. Trust your feeling and proceed to recapitulate it in the heat of the moment.

What About Recapitulating with Other People?

It is wonderful if you can have companions on the journey. Obviously, each one of them would be making his own trip, but you all would have the privilege of sharing with other travelers at some point on the road.

The procedure is nearly the same as has been described for one person. The main difference is that there is going to be more energy in motion. This is good for those who are traveling "in the rear part of the train" because they may be pulled by the ones going ahead. There is no specific way to do this—it just happens. It is simply the way the energy reacts.

The ritual or preparation exercises will be done together. Actually, you may do almost everything together, except the work with the list and the work inside the box. The boxes are located in the same room, near each other. Do not worry about making noise during your work. If your recapitulation becomes intense, it is not going to disturb your companions. On the contrary: your energy in motion is going to make it easier for them to put their own energy in motion.

It should be obvious that working with others makes no sense if you get together in any way that would not be respectful. Accept working with others only if they and you are going to share a real commitment for the task. Once you start the challenge, there is no way to go back and withdraw from the battle.

What Am I Doing Wrong?

"I have tried to do the recapitulation by following the steps described here, but I can't keep focused, I can't relive the events, and I don't have a feeling that seems to be recapitulation."

This kind of reaction is very common at the beginning of the process. You feel that you can't succeed at all; you feel that the techniques are not working for you. You should be ready for this effect and not give up—most people feel this way in their first attempts. Even if they follow all the steps, they are left with the impression that they are not able to enter into recapitulation. Actually, the initial process as I have seen it happen for most people could be described as follows:

1. You try to recapitulate following the techniques, but you don't do the steps thoroughly. Especially for the steps of reliving, intensification, and decision making, most people skip the parts that they feel are strange or ridiculous. In this stage you feel that you are not succeeding in recapitulating.
2. You are urged not to give up, to try again, but this time to follow all the indications thoroughly, no matter how strange they might seem. At this point you are not skipping any parts of the steps. You notice some difference, but you still feel that the recapitulation doesn't trigger. The feeling of not succeeding in your goal may continue.
3. You are urged to keep trying. All this is normal at the beginning stage. Finally, by practicing more, the recapitulation is triggered! Now you discover how it feels to recapitulate and how strong and powerful this technique is. Congratulations—and keep going until you complete the recapitulation of your life!

Based on my experience I would say that the average amount of time it takes for people to enter into recapitulation is three to four days into a fifteen-night recapitulation program. In the three-day intensive seminar program, the participants learn to recapitulate under our guidance. They follow our instructions, step by step, and everybody is recapitulating the same kind of event at the same time. In this program the latest that most people enter into the recapitulation experience is day two, during the third segment of recapitulating events. As I said, this is just an average—obviously, each person's specific case may be different.

The main point here is this: *Don't give up if you find that the first attempts at recapitulating aren't that "successful." This is normal. Move ahead.*

Can I Change the Ten Steps?

Should I always follow the ten steps exactly as they are described here, or can I be flexible and change them a bit according to the needs of the moment?

This is an important question, and provides a very appropriate to finish the book. Answer: In the beginning you should follow the steps exactly as they are described, even those that you might think are exaggerated, ridiculous, or strange. Doing so will help you halt the ego's resistance and, most important, will help you stop the domination of the rational mind. This is the rule for the period of time when your body is learning how to recapitulate: Follow the steps thoroughly.

Once the recapitulation process is triggered, you will notice that you are able to pass from one step to the next more smoothly. It takes less time to focus on recapitulation as you use your initial breathing technique. You may even skip the step of seeing the event and jump directly into reliving it. Decision making becomes a less verbal action, because your body gets used to making the energy movement that is the actual energetic command. With enough practice, the step-by-step procedure becomes a natural process wherein the steps are not separated. The summary or main content of the process is reliving, healing, and reinforcing (through the liberated acts). Just that: reliving, healing, and reinforcing the healing. When this process is natural for you, you may finish the recapitulation of your entire life within a few years, months, or weeks, depending on how intensive your personal program is. At this point recapitulation becomes part of your collection of personal resources. It becomes what it has always been: a natural process of energetic self-healing, at your disposal whenever you need it.

My Last Comment

I have done the best I could to convince you of the value of practicing recapitulation. I have given you all the support that I have been able to imagine for your adventure. My heart is empty because I have let out everything that was inside and wanting to fly, in relation to recapitulation technology.

The only thing I can do now is wish you a journey full of effort and encounters with your other self and with the Great Spirit. Recapitulation will change your life. Do not dare to engage yourself in such a journey if you are not willing to surrender to the overwhelming mystery of change.

If you do start on the journey, may our brilliant fields of energy shine together in the search for our common destiny.

Appendix A

Table of Examples

This following table contains examples of events from the past that left energetic damage in the energetic bodies of the people who experienced them, together with examples of the routines that were generated as a consequence, the kind of decision making that resulted from the recapitulation process, and the liberated actions that were appropriate for the decisions made.

The examples are presented here with the hope that they may be useful for you when you are trying to sort out what your energetic promises were, what your decisions might be, and what the corresponding notdoings would be. Especially at the beginning, it is not easy to have a clear vision of how to handle these parts of the process. Once you have practiced, it becomes much easier.

Please be aware that the following table is not like a cooking recipe. It does not mean that if you have had a similar event, you should *necessarily* follow the examples of this table in terms of decision making and notdoings. Actually, presenting the events in this fashion is an oversimplification of processes that are much more complex. The table shows one possible way to handle each of the events presented; as with all the contents of this book, the use of your own discernment is always required.

Example	1	2	3
Event (or situation behind the event)	Your father didn't give you affection.	You were caught stealing a relative's money.	You were violently rejected when you wanted to express love.
Energetic Command	"I will not love you. I hate you."	"I am not trustworthy."	"I will not show my feelings to others."
Doing (internal routine)	Keep the distance with your father. Pretend you don't love him.	Your actions ruin the trust that others have in you.	Never say "I love you." Show anger to hide your sadness, to pretend you don't need anyone.
Decision Making	"I accept that I love you without judgment and without asking for reward."	"I give up the promise of not being trustworthy; I will honor the trust that others put in me."	"From now on I will express what I feel to the people I care about—fear will not stop me!"
Not-Doing	Approach your father, embrace him, and express affection for him, without expecting a reward.	Be honest, sometimes confessing lies you have said before, to give a sacred value to being truthful.	Confess your feelings to your relatives, friends, partner, and so on. Grow used to expressing your feelings.

Example	4	5	6
Event (or situation behind the event)	Your first great love left you for someone else, and you were broken-hearted as a result. That feeling of loss has been with you all your life.	Your father used to beat you. He was violent and cold. You have memories of physical aggression.	You were not a physically strong child. You were not good at sports. Other children made fun of you, and your parents didn't help.
Energetic Command	"I will not trust in women [or men] anymore."	"I hate you. I will be rude to others so they won't notice my weakness and hurt me."	"I am a loser. I will not expose myself and allow them to see I am weak."
Doing (internal routine)	You are not able to trust deeply, not able to surrender when making love, not able to give your heart to the person you love.	You are aggressive with others, you shout and beat your kids. You are like a general with your family. You are given to fighting.	You are shy and have no confidence in dealing with the opposite sex. You act as if you can't be loved. You are scared of starting new projects.

Example	4	5	6
Decision Making	"I thank you for the love you gave me. I accept that you had to go. I will see every woman [man] I meet as a new human being. When the moment comes, I will dare to surrender to the mystery of love and trust."	"I forgive you, Father, not because what you did was right but for my own well-being. I release my rancor against you. From now on, I will love children the way I would have liked to be loved by you."	"I accept myself without comparing myself to others. I am alive, strong, and full of life. I will do what I want, and I'll take the risk of winning or losing. Regardless, I will be happy because fear will not stop me."
Not-Doing	Take the risk of love and trust. When you are in love, make love passionately and uninhibitedly with your partner.	Play and be tender with your children. Learn to be a clown for the joy of children in parks, schools, or parties (and charge no fee).	Behave confidently when approaching the opposite sex. Start new activities. Practice sports for joy instead of competition and concern about winning.

Example	7	8
Event (or situation behind the event)	Your parents gave you everything but love. You were wealthy but lonely.	Your mother never approved of what you did. There was always something wrong. She was a perfectionist, and you were never able to please her.
Energetic Command	"If they don't need me, I will not need them. Nobody is important but me. I will not need anyone. Everybody is below me."	"Whatever I do, it will never be enough. I am not good enough."
Doing (internal routine)	You are proud of your money, even if you didn't earn it. You judge others based on material richness. You act and relate to others only from the surface. You pretend you are happy when actually you are miserable.	You always find fault with other people's actions. You are a perfectionist, demanding too much from yourself and from others. You are always unhappy because of your neurotic perfectionism. You try to demonstrate to others how good you are.
Decision Making	"I will not continue to judge people by their material success. I will learn to see the heart; I will value people for what they are and not for what they have. I will show my heart and confess my feelings. I will love others the way I would have liked to be loved."	"I give up trying to be perfect. I will relax and do what I do for the joy of it. I can make mistakes and it's all right. I will stop demanding that others do things the way I think is right. I am just a person. I can make mistakes and it's okay."

Example	7	8
Not-Doing	Dress simply, without ostentation or flaunting of wealth. Make friends with good people who have no money. Perform voluntary social services in poor communities to learn to love without expecting a reward.	Make mistakes on purpose in front of others and stay relaxed.* Practice tolerance and make a nice comment when you see others making mistakes. *Do not exaggerate this, and remember to use common sense.

Opportunities to Grow Together: The AVP Workshops

A VP is an organization for personal and spiritual growth that was born and is based in Mexico. In AVP we believe that every person has already within him- or herself everything that he or she needs to accomplish the challenge of having a worthy life. We do not believe in masters or gurus. We believe in personal responsibility as the only and indispensable requisite for the task of achieving knowledge and freedom.

Because of this, all our workshops, seminars, and written materials are designed in such a way as to avoid dependence. We do not have progressive degrees to ensure future clients.

Our instructors are not charismatic leaders who are going to be at the center of everyone's attention as the important element of your learning process. We believe and practice the Nimomashtic way: teaching yourself. In that spirit, we invite people who want to share the experience of growth, people who are not looking for perfect masters. What we have to offer is our unbending commitment to our path and the experience of having done this work for a long time.

The goals of our work have to do with rescuing our magical side, the other self who is missing in our lives, in order to balance and heal the problems we have as a consequence of trying to rule our lives with only the participation of our rational mind. The freedom of reinventing ourselves, choosing how to be and how to live, is also one of our main aims.

We are not looking for the other side of ourselves just for the sake of doing strange things or because we want to know how this other side feels. We need to rescue our other self for a very simple and pragmatic reason: We cannot have a balanced and healthy life without the participation of our full awareness. Trying to live by taking care of only the tonal is like trying to work with one leg when we have two.

Our workshops, seminars, and self-learning programs are very practice-oriented and are not directed toward intellectual discussions. In these programs you do not need to believe—you just need to do, and only actual experience will give you the knowledge that can change your life for the better.

You can register for and participate in workshops in any order once you have completed "The Jump to the Other Self" workshop, which is the basic experience to help you understand the kind of work we do in AVP. It is the one prerequisite for all other AVP workshops and seminars.

"The Jump to the Other Self" is a workshop whose theme is our nature as dual beings. Instead of just talking about our duality or about the other self, we introduce practical exercises to allow the participants to experience the other self by themselves. This high-impact experience reveals that part of our selves that we are missing in the modern world.

In relation to recapitulation, we offer the "Intensive Workshop of Recapitulation," which currently lasts fifteen days and takes place only in Mexico. We also offer in several countries the three-day "Seminar of Recapitulation." The main difference between these two is that while the intensive seminar deals with doing recapitulation for your entire life, the three-day seminar deals with learning and practicing the recapitulation techniques so that, in addition to recapitulation during the seminar of some of the most decisive moments of your life, you can continue with recapitulation on your own. This seminar provides a "push" into the recapitulation experience because the role of the workshop leader is to help the participants reach beyond their own unconscious resistance, allowing them to truly cross the line between trying to recapitulate and entering real recapitulation.

AVP workshops cover a vast range of themes and goals, including programs for self-training. If you would like more information, please contact us.

Web site: www.toltecas.com

Our mailing address:

AVP

A.P. 12-762

C.P. 03001

Distrito Federal

Mexico

e-mail: avp@toltecas.com

About the Sources
of This Work

This book has been written to support the work of all those looking for avenues to their own freedom, beyond the dictates of ordinary life in our modern societies.

The theme of this book is recapitulation, an ancient process of self-healing through restoring our field of energy from the damage we received in our past. The origin of this technique dates to the time of the ancient Toltecs, but this practice is presented here in its modern form, as created and developed by me and collaborators of AVP Mexico throughout thirteen years of practice and research.

Although some of Carlos Castaneda's works have together been one influential source for this work, it should be made clear that this is an entirely independent work, created and developed by me and all those involved with AVP workshops around the world. While many valuable aspects of the books of Castaneda have been an inspiration for a significant part of my work, it is also true that there are many differences between his work and mine in terms of goals and procedures. Any careful reader of our respective books will easily discern this.

Regarding the specific subject of this book—recapitulation—the influence of the work *The Eagle's Gift* by Carlos Castaneda can be found in the design of part of the AVP Ten-Steps Technique for Recapitulation as well as in the use of some terms, concepts, and expressions. On the other hand, the research, design, goals, procedures, and practical experience from which this work was created are mine.

As I have always made clear in my books, workshops, and seminars, Carlos Castaneda has never been involved with my work, other than as a source of inspiration for parts of my research. My encounters with him in person took place when I was part of the audiences of his semiprivate presentations in Mexico City more than fifteen years ago. He has not been my teacher or my role model in any way. On the contrary, while there are many proposals in Castaneda's work that I found valuable in my quest, it is also true that there are others that I consider obstacles to a sane quest for personal growth and freedom. As with the work of any author, it is important to apply personal criteria and common sense.

The fundamental influence and guide for my work, including this book, is the Toltec tradition that has been kept alive in the mountains of northern Mexico by the surviving Toltecs with whom I have been related and about whom I have written in my previous books.

Whether or not we agree with many of the ideas, doings, or purposes— implicit or explicit—in Castaneda's works and personal behavior, it is clear that his books have affected many of his readers, including me, in positive ways. In my case, his earlier books inspired me to search for new practices such as recapitulation and gave me a push to continue with old challenges such as diving into indigenous knowledge. His works also provided us with a new language to deal with the quest of our hidden self—*second attention, stopping the internal dialogue, self-importance,* and many other terms are going to remain attached to his name for a long, long time.

I feel it is important that we do not forget that his work was not solely his creation, even if it is true that he invented don Juan as a character, as more and more people are accepting nowadays. He was nourished by the ancient quest of our indigenous grandparents, the Toltecs, the Maya, and their predecessors, the Teotihuacáns and Olmecs. They were the ones who discovered for the world the dual nature of human beings and the dual nature of reality. They were the ones who coined words such as *tonal*— for the normal awareness and the ordinary reality—and *nagual*—the secret side of both human beings and the world that surrounds us.

For this reason I want to honor and show gratitude for the genius of the man who was able to attract the attention of millions of readers to the quest for the dual nature of human beings and reality. But even more, I want to honor and thank those indigenous peoples of the past and the present who were and are the inspiration for the quest of Castaneda and for the quest of those millions of women and men enamored of mystery and freedom.

Finally, whatever work we do that helps us move closer to our true nature allows us to be closer to the Great Spirit that gives life to and connects all the existing beings in the universe. The *work* does not belong to anyone, but instead to the Spirit itself, because everything comes from and goes back to that sacred source.

About the Author

After the wonder of his first encounters with indigenous peoples, Victor Sanchez set out to study academic anthropology. From there he returned to the indigenous world and discovered *anti-anthropology,* an attitude of investigation that places emphasis on the human experience in the encounter with otherness, rather than on intellectual reports that reduce reality to the narrow limits of a theoretical framework. From his twenty years of experience in different fields he has produced a form of personal growth called the Art of Living Purposefully, or the New Toltequity.

From his adventures in the natural world (crossing deserts, jungles, and mountains, and exploring communication with whales and dolphins), he sees the encounter with nature as the ideal space within which to reencounter our natural self and find the answers to our fundamental questions. In his work, this encounter is not an intellectual approximation or an ecology of the mind. It is participation of the body and an ecology that comes from the heart, which is expressed through a way of living.

From his experience with indigenous groups in Mexico—survivors who keep alive the spiritual traditions of the ancient Toltecs—he brings us a message: We are children of the sun. Our nature is to shine and, as double beings, we must reincorporate into our daily lives the awareness of the other self that lies hidden inside us, waiting to be resurrected in order to show us the Toltec we all unknowingly carry within.

The proposals of Victor Sanchez are not mere affirmations whose existence terminates with the pages of a book or in the realm of thoughts. Rather they are an open invitation to the practices that can incorporate these ideas as a living substance into our daily experience. The workshops and seminars he has given through the years express clearly that his message is not directed toward the sphere of thinking. Instead it points to the realm of experiences.

Above all, his work is an invitation for us to get away from thinking and talking about knowledge, and instead to begin to live knowledge in our body and heart, within the context of our everyday life and people. It is an invitation to take our own responsibility rather than to wait for someone else to take it for us. And this is because what we are searching for is inside us. The only prerequisite is to recover the essential experience of listening to ourselves, penetrating that inner space where the Spirit dwells, the place from which it speaks to us without words, through what the author calls *silent knowledge*.

In *The Teachings of Don Carlos*, the author relates the testimony of his experience with developing and applying a practical methodology inspired by the books of Carlos Castaneda, a process that was enabled by his experience among the indigenous peoples of the Toltec lineage.

In *Toltecs of the New Millennium*, Sanchez narrates his experience among the Toltec "survivors." From an anti-anthropological perspective he opens the door to that parallel universe where the Wirrarika dwell, thus supplying a living testimony to indigenous knowledge.

Now, with *The Toltec Path of Recapitulation*, the author shares a powerful technique that is the shamanic alternative to therapies such as psychoanalysis and other Western models that look for the relief of traumas of the past through working with the mind.

Currently, Victor Sanchez continues his experiences among the surviving Toltecs. He has accomplished the commitment he made to the elders and the *marakames* of the Sierra Wirrarika on November 15, 1993: to submit a written register of a portion of the Wirrarika spiritual tradition in a book directed not toward the general public, but to these indigenous communities, thus rectifying the existing practice among anthropologists and writers of neglecting to return the fruits of their labors to the communities in which their investigations are carried out. The objective in gathering a written testimony of the traditions has been to contribute to their preservation and to provide the new generations of Wirrarika, who are in the process of learning to read, with books that relate to and speak of their own traditions, rather than only those of the Tewaris (nonindigenous peoples). By the end of 1999, Sanchez officially delivered two hundred copies of the book *Recopilación de elementos de la tradición Wirrarika*, which has not been published anywhere else, to the indigenous authorities in the Wirrarika region where he has been working all these years.*

Aside from his spending time in the indigenous world, Victor Sanchez writes books and offers conferences, workshops, and seminars around the world. Starting in 2000, he and his team began pursuing a new stage of experience—introducing their work to the corporate world, in preparation for the increasing strength of corporations around the globe and thus a greater imperative for their representatives to be given the opportunity for increased awareness. To further this, the author is

*This general geographical name of the location of the Wirrarika community is used here to preserve the secrecy of their location in an effort to avoid promoting the increasing flow of nonindigenous people into their remote communities, which, in the view of their elders and shamans, may well endanger the survival of their way of life.

working with corporate leaders who are interested in promoting self-realization among their employees, contributing to the peaceful coexistence of people, and increasing global awareness.

In all arenas Victor Sanchez is working to create a bridge that allows people to nourish themselves with the magic that is preserved among indigenous communities of Toltec descent, a magic that holds the most priceless and powerful treasures ever generated by human experience on this earth: the knowledge of otherness.

Also by Victor Sanchez

The Teachings of Don Carlos

Practical Applications of the Works
of Carlos Castaneda

VICTOR SANCHEZ

Millions of readers of Carlos Castaneda have long enjoyed the teachings of don Juan Matus, the Yaqui shaman from northern Mexico. Now, thanks to the practical techniques offered here, you can apply these teachings to your everyday life.

"I was struck by the clarity, intensity, and insight of Sanchez's words. . . . He comprehends the nature of magical transformation."

Gnosis

ISBN 1-879181-23-1 • $14.00 pb

Books of Related Interest by Bear & Company

*The Teachings of Don Carlos: Practical Applications of the Works of
Carlos Castaneda* by Victor Sanchez
ISBN 1-879181-23-1 • $14.00 pb

Toltecs of the New Millennium by Victor Sanchez
ISBN 1-879181-35-5 • $14.00 pb

*Don Juan and the Art of Sexual Energy: The Rainbow Serpent
of the Toltecs* by Merilyn Tunneshende
ISBN 1-879181-63-0 • $15.00 pb

Mastery of Awareness: Living the Agreements
by Doña Bernadette Vigil
ISBN 1-879181-61-4 • $14.00 pb

Secrets of Mayan Science and Religion by Hunbatz Men
ISBN 0-939680-63-7 • $12.00 pb

Walking on the Wind: Cherokee Teachings for Harmony and Balance
by Michael Garrett
ISBN 1-879181-49-5 • $14.00 pb

Medicine of the Cherokee: The Way of Right Relationship
by J. T. Garrett and Michael Garrett
ISBN 1-879181-37-1 • $14.00 pb

These and other Inner Traditions • Bear & Company titles are available at many fine
bookstores. To order directly from the publisher, please call 1-800-246-8648 or mail a
check or money order for the total amount, payable to Inner Traditions, plus $4.50 ship-
ping for the first book and $1.00 for each additional book to:

Inner Traditions • Bear & Company
P.O. Box 388, Rochester, VT 05767
1-800-246-8648 • *Be sure to request a free catalog*
Visit our Web site at www.InnerTraditions.com